letter to jimmy

(On the twentieth anniversary of your death)

Alain Mabanckou

Translated from the French by Sara Meli Ansari

Soft Skull Press | Berkeley
An Imprint of Counterpoint

Library of Congress Cataloging-in-Publication Data

ISBN 978-1-59376-601-6
Mabanckou, Alain, 1966– author.
[Lettre à Jimmy. English]
Letter to Jimmy : on the twentieth anniversary of your death / Alain Mabanckou ;
translated by Sara Meli Ansari.
    pages cm
ISBN 978-1-59376-601-6 (paperback)
1. Baldwin, James, 1924-1987—Criticism and interpretation. 2. African Ameri-
cans in literature. I. Ansari, Sara Meli, translator. II. Title.
PS3552.A45Z7813 2014
818'.5409—dc23
            2014022425
Cover design by quemadura
Interior design by Neuwirth & Associates, Inc.

SOFT SKULL PRESS
An imprint of COUNTERPOINT
2560 Ninth Street, Ste. 318
Berkeley, CA 94710
www.softskull.com
www.counterpointpress.com

Printed in the United States of America

Distributed by Publishers Group West

10 9 8 7 6 5 4 3 2 1

But more important than that, perhaps, was the relationship between American Negroes and Africans and Algerians in Paris . . . . It didn't demand any spectacular degree of perception to realize that I was treated, insofar as I was noticed at all, differently from them because I had an American passport. I may not have liked this fact: but it was a fact . . . if I were an African, [Paris] would have been a very different city to me.

JAMES BALDWIN,
in an interview from December 29, 1961,
in *Conversations with James Baldwin*, University Press
of Mississippi, 1989.

contents

foreword

the Santa Monica wanderer

As the seagulls desert Santa Monica State Beach, and a small boat pitches on the waves in the distance, I sense your presence as I do each time I wander here. I fix my eyes on the horizon, watch the fading of the sun, and I stretch myself out on the sand. The clouds seem to form shadowy figures—today an elderly woman with an unsteady step.

I want to forget the world around me: the hubbub of the street, images of movies I have recently seen, the books still open on my desk.

In truth I envy the wanderer I see at the other end of Santa Monica beach, a gray beard he has not shaven in years falling to his chest. Never has a stranger so fully captured my imagination, prompting me to trail him, as if I expected him to reveal the key to the mysteries that confront me when I read your work. I cannot stop myself from wondering about his life, with the secret hope that one day I will find a way to speak to him about you. I know that he will take the time to listen to me; he spends his day conversing with invisible beings, throwing his head back in laughter for no apparent reason, urinating at the foot of a tree, forgetting to zip his pants, getting irritated by a flock of gulls, then sits down on his shoes, worn through from wandering. But the strangest thing, Jimmy, is that he will build colossal sand castles, where he must dream of ruling as king of his own fantasies, with his court, his family, his subjects and his guard. Then suddenly he will demolish his kingdom with a nervous kick of the foot, and again return to being a wreck of a man.

Dejected, he will roam over toward the great Ferris wheel of Pacific Park, which ordinarily draws the Santa Monica tourists. I have seen him remove a bowl from a pocket in his ragged clothes and beg until nightfall. He seems like a character lifted straight from the pages of one of your novels!

It is to him, to this wanderer, that I dedicate this letter.

1.

a brave mother, and a father
who did not love himself

The photo is in front of me, hanging on the wall. Your eyes are the first to capture my attention. Those big eyes—prominent on your face, that once mocked your father, unaware that they would later peer into souls, or that they would pierce through the darkest part of humanity, before closing forever—still hold their power to search deeply, even from the next life.

Eyes lifted skyward, eyebrows raised high. What are you thinking at the moment the photographer focuses his lens on you?

The picture is in black and white.

It looks to me today like an extension of your characters who share your voice, your mannerisms, your laughter, your anger, your exasperation. I linger in vain over your half-smile, a smile no doubt interrupted by the flash as you lifted your head up to the right; I know its mystery will remain.

You wear a white collared shirt with long sleeves, your black tie loosened, a cigarette wedged between your index and middle fingers. Each crease on your face casts a spell. Studying you this way, I sometimes imagine that we are building a dialogue, and that you are listening to me, entertained by my unanswerable questions.

When I turn over the photo—it has become a reflex—I read aloud the few words I have scribbled there: "What's the weather like in heaven, Jimmy?"

* * *

The photo carries me back to the 1920s, to the front of a public building, Harlem Hospital, in New York City. Emma Berdis Jones is twenty-eight years old at the time. On the 2nd of August 1924, she delivers a child out of wedlock, who is, as a result, illegitimate—a bastard. And you, you enter the world through the back door. Your eyes are not bothered by the light; they make out the environment, recording for later the wounds of a torn and quartered society built on a patchwork of "ethnicities." Some people dominate, direct, decide. Others just endure, abide the ghetto borders, and do not have the right to sit next to the white man on public transportation . . .

Emma Berdis Jones is certain that anyone who comes to this world through the back door will rise up one day. However, at this time in her life, her existence is as unstable as it can be. She takes odd jobs. More often than not, she gets placed as a housekeeper. After your birth, she tells herself that her days of wandering are finally over: she left behind Deal Island, Maryland, then Philadelphia, before dropping anchor in New York. It is there that she met David Baldwin, a man who could have been her father, but who agrees to become yours. This is a man whose oldest daughter, from a first marriage, is older than your mother, while his youngest son, Samuel, is eight years your senior. This is the man who gives you your name. And Emma, to whom you dedicate your masterpiece, *No Name in the Street*, has only one obsession: to give you a name.

What is a name, after all? Almost nothing. But a name says everything, and introduces us to the world.

We wear it with pride if we can attach it to a glorious past. It becomes an embarrassment when it suggests "illegitimacy." You would not keep your mother's name, Jones, for very long, since in 1927, three years after your birth, she marries David Baldwin.

On that day, you become James Arthur Baldwin . . .

You would keep this name until the end of your days, without ever rejecting or changing it, unlike other stars of African-American history: Malcolm Little (who became

Malcolm El Shabbaz, then Malcolm X) or Marcellus Cassius Clay, Jr. (who became Muhammad Ali), or the playwright and poet Everett LeRoi Jones (who became Amiri Baraka).

By keeping the name "Baldwin," you are aware of perpetuating despite yourself a lineage forged of lurid relationships, domination, whipping, and slavery. You are, in reality, just the "Negro" of some Baldwin, a "white slave owner who, several centuries earlier, had entered into possession of one of the ancestors of David."[1]

Between those who advocate a return to roots—captivated by Pan-Africanist leaders like Marcus Garvey—and black Americans who replace their family name with an X to signal their affiliation with the Nation of Islam, you identify your situation as even more complex because of your double illegitimacy: the intimate illegitimacy, through your unknown biological father; and the historic, distant one, a product of slavery. The letter X, in vogue at the time, represents the unknown in an equation that has yet to be solved. It is the symbol of a very long path to be rebuilt, that leads all the way back to the remote village on the "dark continent," where your African ancestors were captured and torn from their lands by slave traders: "The American Negro is a unique creation; he has no counterpart anywhere, and no predecessors. The Muslims react to this fact by referring to the Negro as 'the so-called American Negro' and substituting for the names inherited from slavery the letter 'X.'"[2]

Through the name Baldwin, you want to attach a meaning to your descent from a slave owner—and a slave—of history's transgressions, the violence and humiliation suffered: "I am called Baldwin because I was either sold by my African tribe or kidnapped out of it into the hands of a white Christian named Baldwin, who forced me to kneel at the foot of the cross."[3]

*   *   *

Were you born on the right side of things? Do you have the right skin color?

You admire your mother, a "small courageous woman," Emma, the epitome of endurance, courage and self-sacrifice. She has nine children to care for, and she fears that she cannot manage to raise them because of the street, because of "this Harlem ghetto" where "rents are 10 to 58 per cent higher than anywhere else in the city; food, expensive everywhere, is more expensive here and of an inferior quality; and now that the war is over and money is dwindling, clothes are carefully shopped for and seldom bought."[4]

The Harlem in which you live is a pile of hovels, a den of prostitution and of drugs, tuberculosis, alcoholism and crime. Above all, it is the scene of the most appalling racial atrocities that often unfold under police watch, when they themselves are not committing the acts or are not pulling the strings behind the curtains. Emma Berdis Jones warns you against "the street" that corrupts, derails and perverts.

The feeling there is of an abandoned neighborhood, separate from the rest of New York. And when riots erupt on March 19, 1935, after the murder of a black man by a white police officer—several thousand men take it out on white-owned businesses, causing a good portion of the middle-class to flee the neighborhood—you see that, despite the widespread indignation, political figures merely make endless speeches, set up committees, and tear down a few hovels to replace them with housing projects. They still do not take concrete and effective steps to ". . . right the wrong, however, without expanding or demolishing the ghetto." And this futile activity seems to you "about as helpful as make-up to a leper."[5]

An entire universe exists between the ghetto and the heart of the city, situated only a few blocks apart.

When you go to the public library on 42nd Street, you get the feeling of entering another world. In this area, most people are homeowners. And they make sure you know it, you outsiders, you people of color. If necessary, the police will also see to it that you understand.

Under these circumstances, you and your brothers conclude that Emma is too inclined to absolution and indulgence toward her fellow man: the exact opposite of David Baldwin. She is the one who reminds you, "You have lots of brothers and sisters . . . You don't know what's going to happen to them. So you're to treat everybody like your brothers and sisters. Love them." [6]

Who are these siblings in need of protection? Barbara, Gloria, Paula, Ruth—your sisters. And your brothers: Samuel, George, Wilmer and David. Your father's obsession with the name David is obvious: not only is it his name, but he already had a son with this name from a previous union at the time he married your mother. He then gives the same name to one of your younger brothers. One might say that yours is "the house of David."

While Emma embodies security and familial protection, David is distant and consumed by his religious faith. Although he is a factory worker, he proudly dons a dark jacket and brushed black hat every Sunday. Then, with a Bible tucked under his arm, he preaches in the abandoned warehouses of Harlem.

To suffer through everything without complaint, is Emma Berdis a saint?

"I would not describe her as a saint, which is a terrible thing to do. I think she is a beautiful woman . . . When I think about her, I wonder how in the world she did it, how she managed that block, those streets, that subway, nine children. No saint would have gotten through it! But she is a beautiful, a fantastic woman. She saved all our lives." [7]

So what happened to your biological father?

You do not know him, and you will never know him. This mystery will be one of the greatest torments of your adolescence. The shadows cast by this dark cloud scatter themselves through most of your writing. Your friend and biographer David Leeming explains how much the idea of "illegitimacy" remained a constant preoccupation for you, to the point that it can be detected in the titles of several of your books: *Nobody Knows My Name*, *Stranger in the Village* . . ."[8]

Leeming nevertheless specifies that although the search for a father haunted you, it was not just for your biological father—you consider David Baldwin to be your own father, and when you mention him, you express a certain pride in bearing his name. In fact, as your biographer points out, you dreamed of a father who would accompany you on your long path to writing, and in your work as a preacher, to which David Baldwin was particularly attached. But starting in your adolescence and at the time you became a pastor, an even more complicated relationship developed between the two of you, as another of your biographers, Benoît Depardieu, explains: "By entering religion, in becoming a pastor-preacher, young James was turning toward another father, God the Father, and in so doing he hoped not only to escape from David Baldwin, his stepfather, but also to take his place by defying him and surpassing him in his own domain. This desire to compete with the father and to defeat him demonstrates a common oedipal complex."[9]

David Baldwin cannot imagine an existence without his work as a preacher. This is all the more true since he sees before him every day the stigma of what he holds to be the greatest injustice: his own mother who lives with you, Barbara Ann Baldwin, was a former slave. Every black American is linked to the history of slavery. But Barbara Ann Baldwin is there in the flesh, and her history is not confined to textbooks; it is written across the downcast eyes of the old woman.

David Baldwin draws his entire family into his religious zeal. He has a rigid idea of Biblical teachings. Is it this rigidity that persuades him to have such a large family, since the Bible applauds fertility and mankind's continuous reproduction?

In one way or another, it is your relationship with this man that will inform your views on American society and on interracial relations. You feel a sense of urgency to understand what feeds his hatred of the Other. Deep down, even if you devote yourself to admiring this hard and rigid being, you do not share the same understanding of the world, his view of the black man's place in the world, nor his unwavering hostility toward the white man. The "murder" of the father will be symbolized by the "hatred" you harbor toward him. But does

David Baldwin even love himself? He is not happy,
to say the least. Never has anyone despised himself so
much, you will tell yourself. He goes so far as to blame
himself for the color of his skin. He will spend his life
apologizing for it in all of his actions and believing
that religion is the only path to salvation. In his mind,
Leeming reminds us, even if the "white demon" does not
recognize him as a human being in this world, God the
Omnipotent, in His goodness and fairness, will rectify
the injustice. This explains his antipathy toward IRS
agents, landlords, and all whites who, in his mind, exercise a certain abusive power over blacks. However, he
gathers through his daily reading of the Holy Book that
the power of the white world is ephemeral, and that God
will come one day to set the record straight. And on that
day, the believers, the true believers, will have the upper
hand over the non-believers.

This Manichean understanding commits him to absolute distrust. Since the world has always been corrupt,
there can never be any cooperation between whites and
blacks—the latter will always lose in that fool's errand.
As a result, the few whites who ever cross the threshold
of your home are social workers or bill collectors. These
public employees are not protected from the fury of the
master of the house, although your mother still scurries
around to receive them. David Baldwin, on the other
hand, will bellow about the "violation of his domestic

privacy," and you all fear that his pride will drive him to commit the unthinkable.

* * *

During your childhood, you have countless opportunities to witness the extent to which your father distrusts the white man, whoever he may be, even if he has the best intentions in the world. For David Baldwin, it is not only the white man who is bad: all white people are, without exception.

You tell the story of a white school-teacher who had to confront your suspicious father when she got the notion to take you to the theater. You were nine or ten years old, and you had just written a play that the school-teacher, devoted and admiring as she was, had already put on at school. She believed that in order to complement your education in drama, you had to live the theater, watch actors perform, feel the emotion of the audience. But at home, the theater, as well as movies and books, synonyms of perversion and of the grasp of the "white demon," were forbidden. So was jazz, the "music of bought Negros," that fascinates men of color who are caught in the trap of the white demon. David Baldwin took the invitation to the theater as an insult, a challenge to his authority, and an intrusion by a malicious force into the house of God. He has the habit of repeating a citation from the Bible: "As my house and myself, we will serve the Lord." Never mind that he is incapable of meeting the needs of his family, or that his sons are reduced to engaging in an activity that young black men of the time could not shake: they were shoe-shiners, whose "pathetic" image was further perpetuated through advertisements. It was an image as moving as that of a "darky bootblack doing a buck and wing to the clatter of condescending coins."[10] Moreover, David Baldwin does not hold it against his wife for working as a maid in white homes. If money does not have a smell, one might add here, too, that it does not have a color . . .

That a white woman should offer to take one of David Baldwin's sons to the theater is nevertheless enough to ignite his indignation. He immediately called into question the school-teacher's interest in his son, convinced that behind her motivation and zeal there were some diabolical games at play: the white man is always out to get the black man. It was therefore against your father's will that the school-teacher should help you experience the emotion of a theatrical performance for the first time.

Would David Baldwin have had the same reaction if the school-teacher had been a woman of color? Certainly not. You would hold on to these words for the rest of your life: ". . . he warned me that my white friends in high school were not really my friends, and that I would see, when I was older, how white people would do anything to keep a Negro down. Some of them could be nice, he admitted, but none of them were to be trusted and most of them were not even nice. The best thing was to have as little to do with them as possible. I did not feel this way and I was certain, in my innocence, that I never would."[11]

* * *

David Baldwin is black, and does not realize that he is beautiful, you point out. You add that he dies with a fierce conviction of his ugliness. No doubt overcome by his own frustration, he makes tasteless jokes about your "ugliness" and your "big eyes" to the point of saying that you are the most unfortunate child he has ever laid eyes on. You were affected for a long time by his idea of ugliness. At a young age, we end up accepting what is said about us, especially when it comes from adults. It remains this way until something comes along to contradict those early notions, to make things right, even if only superficially.

You study yourself. You think about these eyes, so prominent on your face, that you inherited from Emma Berdis Jones, and you ask yourself if your father might not be right. What purpose could these big eyes serve?

Why do they protrude so much? Had Mother Nature really punished you, or was she distinguishing you in some way? Desperation grips you. How many times have you told the story that made you discover that there is always something "uglier" than oneself in this world? In fact, when you were still just a child, you saw in the street, from a window in your apartment, a woman with eyes even more prominent than yours, with, on top of everything, and as if nature had had it in for her, over-sized lips. You conclude that she is uglier than you. You run to tell your mother, to console her, to prove to her that you no longer have any reason to be tormented by this physical detail, and that human beings are judged by the quality of their souls . . .

In fact, when David Baldwin focuses on your supposed ugliness, when he makes it the subject of his frequent tormenting, he hits your weak spot, and from it you draw a painful conclusion about the consequences of being a "bastard": through his behavior, your step-father is indirectly attacking your biological father . . . This leads you to regret yourself, and to reproach this unknown man, your biological father, for having approached Emma, and having transmitted to you her physical disgrace; impossible to erase, obvious at first glace. From that point forward, when you rest your big eyes on him, you imagine a pathetic being—a very old, frozen statue . . .

Despite his despicable character that suggests David

Baldwin is completely cold to his family—to the point that you describe him as "a monster in the house. Maybe he saved all kinds of souls, but he lost all of his children, every single one of them," a monster experiencing a visceral aversion toward the white race—you also remember moments where this man seemed to you at last like a devoted father: human, feeling, attentive, managing the best he could for his family. You remember a time when your mother would carry you on her shoulders, and David Baldwin would be walking beside her, smiling at you. You remember, too, the image of this old man offering you candy.

But very quickly you recall the harsh reality of your father who pronounces you good-for-nothing, and does not hesitate to beat you to a pulp when you lose the change you are given to buy kerosene for heating the family home. Did this hateful man prepare you for life's battles? You say your father ". . . was perhaps too old to have as many children in a strange land as he had. The world was changing so fast, and he was in such trouble that he could not change with it . . . He had nine children he could hardly feed. His pain was so great that he translated himself into silence, rigidity . . . sometimes into beating us and finally into madness . . . Without him I might be dead because knowing his life and his pain taught me how to fight."[14]

This man sets up barriers between himself and others.

He has difficulty maintaining close relationships with his friends who, one by one, distance themselves from him little by little. He is sick for years, but the illness from which he suffers is far from being physical: everything happens in his head, in his mind, to the point that you can no longer grasp the internal pain of a being who slides into the most extreme paranoia, stands in front of the window for hours reciting prayers and humming religious songs. It is in this distant, celestial world that he feels best. From this point forward, his hatred is out in the open. One might even say that he resents his nine children, resents their entry into this repulsive world that does not acknowledge him and that the Lord will make disappear. The paranoia reaches its peak when he begins to refuse to eat at home, convinced that his own family is plotting to poison him . . .

* * *

You are forced to take the place of your "unfit," gruff, austere father, distrusting of his own family. You help your mother in her difficult role as mother and head of household, without asking yourself whether this role should fall instead into the hands of Samuel, David Baldwin's son from his previous marriage and several years your senior. Still, you marvel at his courage, which he displayed when he saved you from drowning, for example . . . Would this episode itself earn you the name "Moses," who wrote the story of Israel and led his people out of Egypt to deliver them from slavery? Perhaps you, too, have a mission on this Earth, and this mission is passed to you through the knowledge of God, and through the freedom of writing.

Being saved by Samuel marks you, and you bring this up in *No Name in the Street.* The figure of this half-brother would run through *Go Tell It on the Mountain* and again in *Tell Me How Long the Train's Been Gone,* then in *Just Above My Head* . . . The importance of the brother is magnified, his love nearly Christ-like, his arms protective, pulling you to life while the water is trying to swallow you whole . . . .

In the end, isn't life, too, a vast wave that threatens to wash away the home if the father shuts his family out? Because you shoulder nearly the entire burden of father of the house, you become the one to whom the other children turn. You are a savior in your own right. Most of your biographers describe the same image of you from this period: a book in one hand, while tending to one of your brothers or sisters with the other.

David Baldwin knows that there is nothing more he can do. He knows that he cannot slow down your rush toward independence, nor distract your gaze from the page any more than he can stop your frequent visits to the neighborhood public library, or your increasing distance from religion. For him this is a failure. Until this point, to his great joy, you still belonged to the movement of young preachers, and had preached on countless occasions. You were preaching from the age of fourteen in Baptist churches. It was what David Baldwin wanted. This paternal wish comes through in the introduction to *Go Tell It On the Mountain*: "Everyone had always said that John would be a preacher when he grew up, just like his father. It had been said so often that John, without ever thinking about it, had come to believe it himself."

At fourteen years of age, you are considered a good preacher, and very inspired. You become aware of the power of the word. From high on the pulpit, the faith of an entire population hangs from your lips. These black women, men and children are convinced that the words you speak come through your mouth from the Almighty. You know the Bible by heart, and the rhetoric and poetry you breathe into your sermons further inspire the audience, won over by your preaching.[15]

Until that time, the church had been your refuge. You believe it is the only place that can save you from the cruelty of the street. You think of how, in Harlem, police officers stop you, search you; they try to get a rise out of you by yelling insults about your background, the sexuality of black men, even leaving you unconscious in an abandoned lot. It is a violence from which age will not protect you, since already at thirteen, when you are making your way down Fifth Avenue toward the public library on 42nd Street, a policeman shouts at you, "Why don't you niggers stay uptown where you belong?"[16]

Young people your age are wrong, you believe, not to seek shelter in the house of the Lord. You encounter a number of these young, lost souls, given to debauchery, on a daily basis. It is mostly the metamorphosis of the girls and boys you see in choir practice at church that stuns you. They grow and their features change. The girls "give off heat," their chests swell and their hips become round. The boys drink, smoke and discover the pleasures of the flesh. You imagine what you will be like, what you will become when your body has changed, too, and when your voice becomes deeper. You are wracked with anxiety: will you find yourself in the company of "the most depraved individuals of this world?"[17] Your biggest fear is the same one that grips every other black adolescent in the neighborhood: the fear of ending up like a stray dog, no higher on the social ladder than your father: "School therefore began to seem like a game that was impossible to win, so boys stop attending and started looking for work."[18]

Three years more and you would be long gone from the church. Your mind is elsewhere. You can only think of one thing: "to be an honest man and a good writer."[19]

* * *

The reasons for your break with the church? You outline them in *The Fire Next Time.* You begin to understand that religion as it is will not help you obtain love from your fellow man, at least not as far as people of color are concerned. The Bible itself sews a seed of doubt in your mind: "People, I felt, ought to love the Lord because they loved Him, and not because they were afraid of going to Hell. I was forced, reluctantly, to realize that the Bible itself had been written by men, and translated by men out of languages I could not read, and I was already, without quite admitting it to myself, terribly involved with the effort of putting words on paper."[20]

Your disappointment is immense. You saw how churches operated, whether they were white or black churches. You saw that certain ministers became rich at the expense of the faithful, who are always asked to give more: more faith, more charity work, more alms. From the faithful, everything is squeezed out, down to the "last cent," you write. You now know that when you preach, Bible in hand, sweat dripping from your forehead, you are no longer held by the force that used to lift your spirits and persuade the poor that a better world was in store; a Heaven where a spot, even a numbered one, was reserved for them on the right-hand side of the Lord. So on this poor, attentive flock you cast a gaze of compassion and guilt: compassion for the degradation of their daily lives, and guilt for being among those who ignore that reality. You feel as though you are leading them astray: ". . . when I faced a congregation, it began to take all the strength I had not to stammer, not to curse, not to tell them to throw away their Bibles and get off their knees and go home and organize, for example, a rent strike."[21]

How much longer will you be able to hold on?

At 17, you make your decision. And it is a permanent one, since you feel your grievances grow and grow against the Lord you have been serving for three years. You discover that instead of helping you find the peace you desire, religion throws you into profound loneliness. When called upon, you are nothing more than a puppet, a kind of messenger who goes against the best interests of his people. They are hungry, and you promise them riches in another world. They have no home, and you assure them that God will provide for them.

Faced with such realizations, your criticisms of the Holy Book are unforgiving. This book had helped brand an eternal curse onto the skin of the black man: "I was aware of the fact that the Bible had been written by white men. I knew that according to many Christians, I was a descendent of Ham, who had been cursed, and that I was therefore predestined to be a slave."[22]

* * *

Your "hatred" toward David Baldwin evolves into forgiveness the day that you see him dying on his hospital bed. He is a battered man, almost unrecognizable. Do you *have* to continue to be angry with him? With some perspective, you declare: "I imagine one of the reasons people cling to their hates so stubbornly is because they sense, once hate is gone, they will be forced to deal with pain."[23]

At the time of his death, on July 29, 1943, you become aware of the affection you felt for this being. As if looking for reasons to love him, you flip through the family photo album: your stepfather dressed to the nines to preach on a Sunday. It is a sublime image, you think. And you imagine David Baldwin "naked, with war-paint on and barbaric mementos, standing among spears."[24] The impenetrable forehead, those serious features. It is his bitterness that you do not try to explain to yourself, the bitterness that he would take to the grave, "because at the bottom of his heart, he really believed what white people said about him."[25]

When he is hospitalized, you discover that he has a serious case of tuberculosis. But you know that the enemy is not tuberculosis, that it is something else incurable, invisible, far from the diagnosis the doctors have issued from high on their pulpit. The thing that takes David Baldwin away is the "disease of his mind," the one that has been eating away at him from the inside for years: ". . . the disease of his mind helped the disease of his body to destroy him. For the doctors could not force him to eat, either, and, though he was fed intravenously, it was clear from the beginning that there was no hope for him."[26]

2.

the Harlem schoolboy and
the Bible

i am still staring at your photo.

I blow on it lightly to remove the dust, but I do so with the hope that I will awaken the memories enclosed within it. I see a little black boy, a fragile boy, who is crossing the street to his public school while the world is facing the economic crisis of 1929. Wall Street is not far from where this photo was taken. History will always follow in your footsteps.

One person in this institution has an impact on you: Gertrude E. Ayer, the first woman of color to become a public school director in New York City. She reaches out to you, watches out for you, guides you. Gertrude appears in *Go Tell It on the Mountain,* encouraging the young

John Grimes in his studies. However, another woman, a white woman, seems to have helped you, and toward her you display an ingratitude that is surprising, to say the least, as Benoît Depardieu seems to reproach: "Strangely, Orilla Miller, a young, white school-teacher, the other key figure in his elementary school years, remains eternally absent from his fiction. He makes reference to her in several of his essays, but she never appears in any of his novels or short stories in any form whatsoever . . . She undertakes the literary, theatrical, and cinematic education of the young James Baldwin, and even went so far as meeting the Baldwin family. [. . .] Orilla Miller played a particularly important role in shaping the way James understood whites and their world."[27]

It is Orilla Miller who puts on your first play. It is she who endures the wrath of your father when she wants to take you to the theater. But her persistence would win out over David Baldwin's reluctance. She does not stop after the first victory. You visit museums with her, watch films together, share with her a passion for Charles Dickens. Orilla Miller almost becomes a member of your family, and you become a part of hers, where you discuss politics with her husband, Evan Winfield, which broadens your understanding of American society even further. You later admit that you realized, "Whites did not act as they did because they were white, but for other reasons."[28] These social meetings, which, according to Leeming, probably occur unbeknownst to David Baldwin, correct your view of the white world. From this point forward, your view of that world will be based on considering each person individually, and not on a systematic condemnation of an entire group of people. You refuse the simplistic syllogism: a white man kills a black man, and since Paul is white, Paul also kills black men.

Are all white people bad? Black Muslims are inclined to say yes.

Can whites and blacks intermarry? No, would again be the answer from Black Muslims.

And when, many years later, as an adult, you are invited to the home of the head of the Nation of Islam at the time, Elijah Muhammad, he will warn you of the "holocaust" awaiting the white world. This discourse of the black American Muslims brings up bitter memories for you. You cannot erase the looming figure of David Baldwin from your thoughts. You will feel more solidarity than ever with the "other side," destined for Gehenna according to Elijah Muhammad: "I felt I was back in my father's house—as indeed, in a way, I was— and I told Elijah I did not care if white and black people married, and that I had many white friends. I would have no choice, if it came to it, but to perish with them . . ."[29]

From time to time Orilla Miller comes to your house with her sister, Henrietta Miller. She discovers your poverty, the daily burdens and exhaustion of Emma

Berdis Jones, who works like a dog in the kitchen, or in the corner doing the washing with her bare hands. Orilla is moved, and brings clothing for the children. Your admiration is complete: "I loved her, [. . .] with a child's love . . . It is certainly partly because of her, who arrived in my terrifying life so soon, that I never really managed to hate white people . . ."[30]

This woman, who died in 1991, remained close to you until the end of your life.

❖ ❖ ❖

During your secondary school education, two other defining moments arise. They are crucial in your training as a writer. Indeed, when you begin school at the Frederick Douglass junior high school in 1935, you are first captivated by Countee Cullen. He is one of the most influential poets of the Harlem Renaissance. In this school, he teaches French and is also involved in the English department, where another teacher, Herman W. Porter, notices you. The latter is a member of the editorial board of the school's literary journal, *Douglass Pilot*. He has read your essays, praises your talents, and celebrates the refined writing style of a child who is barely thirteen years old. He suggests that you work on the journal, for which you soon become one of the editors-in-chief.

At this time you read and admire two writers. Aside from Charles Dickens, there is Harriet Beecher Stowe, author of *Uncle Tom's Cabin*. This woman of letters will be one of your primary focuses when you define your notion of literature in an article entitled, "Everybody's Protest Novel," in which you will formulate your first "attacks" against your mentor, Richard Wright.

* * *

Entering DeWitt Clinton High School represents a drastic change for you: this public school located in the Bronx enjoys an impressive reputation. To get there, you have to cross all of Harlem, and must therefore take the subway. Still, these commutes take you away for a short while from the confinement of the ghetto. In high school, you meet other adolescents who share your passion for writing. As in your last school, this one also publishes a journal: *The Magpie*. Very quickly you publish articles in it alongside other friends, such as Emile Capouya, Sol Stein and Richard Avedon.

Your former teacher, Countee Cullen, is delighted, and is all the more so when you ask to interview him for the columns of this literary journal, known for having discovered several young American authors. It is Emile Capouya, the son of Spanish immigrants, who introduces you to someone who will become one of your closest friends: the painter Beauford Delaney. He lives in Greenwich Village, the site *par excellence* of artistic culture and bohemian life, on Manhattan's west side. This neighborhood is also known to be a bastion of another culture that defies convention. The Oscar Wilde Bookshop, one of the oldest gay bookshops, for example, would be created here in Greenwich Village in 1967, while at the same time the neighborhood saw the birth of the famous disco group, the Village People. Through its spirit of difference, Greenwich Village becomes the symbol of sexual freedom, particularly for gay culture, starting with the riots that broke out after police attacks on homosexuals, transsexuals, and lesbians at the gay bar, Stonewall Inn, on June 28, 1969. Many use this date to mark the beginning of the struggle for gay rights.

And so, at your wit's end from fighting with your father, you leave home at the age of seventeen—shortly after your break with the church—and you move to Greenwich Village.

* * *

Meanwhile you continue to write more and more. You are sure that your moment has arrived, that it is time to cross the Rubicon. You have to publish in order to be known as an author. Publishers unfortunately reject all your works of fiction. You are not discouraged. As you wait, you decide to read, and to commit yourself to literary criticism. Several years later you collaborate with a photographer on a book about Harlem's storefront churches. Although you receive a Rosenwald Fellowship, this work does not find a publisher, either. It is at this time that you begin to write book reviews, ". . . mostly, as it turned out, about the Negro problem, concerning which the color of my skin made me automatically an expert. Did another book, in company with photographer Theodore Pelatowski, about the store-front churches in Harlem. This book met exactly the same fate as my first—fellowship, but no sale."[31]

Greenwich Village is the site of a burgeoning African-American culture, for young people who want to change the world with their dreams. In this place, daily life resembles their destiny: unstable, wandering, but with no lack of projects. It is a community founded on teamwork. Thanks to Delaney, you develop your artistic awareness, and your passion for music, above all for blues and jazz. Even though you have been imagining it for a while, it is Emile Capouya who convinces you to definitively abandon preaching. You are seventeen.

With only a high school diploma, it is not exactly as if your future is laid out before you. Your craft requires certain sacrifices with which you comply. You take on odd jobs in Greenwich Village until your father's death. As destiny would have it, on the day of your father's passing, on July 29, 1943, your sister Paula is born.

At the Calypso restaurant, where you work as a waiter, you see a lot of people come and go. Most of the biggest writers and artists of the day come to dine here. Your homosexuality is no longer a secret to anyone, and you even come out to your protector, Emile Capouya. During this time, you also begin writing what will become your first novel, *Go Tell It on the Mountain,* and you meet your mentor, Richard Wright, to whom you will submit a number of pages from your manuscript, for the first time. You read everything you can get your hands on. You devour European literature; you are seduced by Balzac, James, Flaubert, and Dostoyevsky, among others . . .

1946 is made the darkest of years with the suicide of your friend Eugene Worth, to whom you never had the chance to reveal your feelings. This dramatic event affects you, and is one of the reasons that speed up your departure from your country.

* * *

In 1948, at the age of twenty-four, you dream of leaving behind everything that is dear to you, of leaving America— your homeland—because, according to you, "it was necessary." You want to follow the trail blazed before you by black American artists and writers no longer willing to endure the abuses inflicted upon them by a system

of politically sanctioned racial segregation. These artists and writers had exported their cultural movement,
the Harlem Renaissance, to Paris, finding in the French
capital and "in the excitement of the cabarets what used
to seduce them in Harlem: the vibrating pulse of new
cultural blood."[32] The wave of these black migrants is
impressive, and includes poets you frequent and novelists
you admire, like William Du Bois and Langston Hughes,
but also stars of the stage, among whom Josephine Baker
is the most famous. France should, theoretically, allow you
to escape from your demeaning status of Black American
Man. However, you do not renounce your country: "I love
America more than any other country in this world, and,
exactly for this reason, I insist on the right to criticize her
perpetually."[33]

And so, some time later, while visiting the United
States after an absence of several years, you are asked
by the media about your adopted country. You make
no concessions to her: you say you could just as easily
live somewhere in Africa, Asia, or in the Third World.
Later, you would, in fact, go on to live in Turkey and
in Switzerland . . . But you have friends in France, even
if this country, according to you, is a "hermetic" place,
often marked by arrogance and "smugness" among its
intellectuals and elite class. Still, you love France more
than ever, and you certainly do not want to speak badly
of a former lover, one who took you in her arms, opened

her doors to you, and did not judge you on your physical appearance.[34]

* * *

People would argue for a long time about the real reasons
behind your "exile" in France. But the truth is that there
is nothing more disheartening that the imprisonment of
a creative person, nothing worse than the feeling that the
world collapsing before you will swallow your dreams in
the end. In the 1940s, the dreams of African-Americans
are targets of a hellish political beast in your homeland.
Living in your country is no "picnic for black people."
The nearest tree could be your gallows without any
form of trial, and meanwhile President Roosevelt faces
opposition in Congress against passing anti-lynching
laws. Overt segregation is commonplace in restaurants,
schools, and in most public places. Your illustrious colleagues who preceded you in France emphasize their
feelings of being writers in their own right, instead of
being people entirely devoid of rights. In France, they
are not considered black: they are artists, first and foremost, writers who capture the attention of the intellectual scene in their adopted country. Gone are the days of
humiliation endured in their own country; the chance
to create in peace, far from racial discrimination, is open
to them.

Later you will admit that you wanted to live in a place where you could write without the feeling of being choked. France became the place where you blossomed, where you truly began to fight with the weapons at your disposal that no one could take away: words.[35]

3.

in the footsteps of
Professor Wright

You arrive in Paris on November 11, 1948.

You live in small hotels, first in the rue du Dragon, then in the rue de Verneuil, not far from the Boulevard Saint-Germain, in rooms often rented to students, whose landlords must be indulgent at the end of the month when it comes time to collect the rent.

You pick up the Bohemian life you had been living in Greenwich village very easily. Reading Henry James enthralls you, while at the same time the people of Saint-Germain bore you. You prefer instead the common people you encounter in cafés, and the North Africans and black Africans with whom you discuss their situation. Nevertheless, as this is the fate of expatriates, you also dine in the homes of your—usually white—fellow countrymen. During this period, you meet Saul Bellow, among others.

Your quest for your own identity explains your participation in these gatherings. You are caught in the trap of frequently spending time with your white fellow Americans. If such a situation helps you to better understand yourself, outside of the issue of race, it cuts you off for some time from French society, whom you frequent very little—you do not yet speak French, which does not help you meet anyone. Meeting other Americans reveals a shocking reality to you: the white American is as lost as you are, and, throughout the course of your discussions, everyone avoids the problem at the core of American society—the question of race. It is far easier to evoke the beauty of the Champs-Elysées or of the Eiffel Tower . . .

Your mentor Richard Wright is already in Paris with his family. When you left New York, you had hidden the address of this venerable writer in your bag, as if it were a good-luck charm. Back home, he had always supported you, even helped you, in becoming an "honest man and a good writer." And to some extent, even if you never clearly admitted this, it is because Wright is in the French capital that you feel comfortable with the idea of going there yourself.

People in the literary circle of black American exiles in Paris—a social circle Michel Fabre calls the "black bank"—know that a young author from Harlem is

arriving. They had heard of him thanks to several articles published in various magazines and literary journals.
Some had known him in Greenwich Village, while others
were set to discover at last this "young, tense man, slight
in stature, with extravagant hand gestures and a facial
expression that could veer from tragic to comic . . ."[36]

This environment reminds you of the circumstances in
which you met Richard Wright in New York, at the end
of 1944. At this time, you are twenty years old. Wright,
at thirty-six, is already famous thanks to his novels, especially *Native Son*. He is the first black American to have
published a bestseller, and the tale that he narrates in
his novel, about Bigger Thomas, a man of color who
murders a rich white woman who is in love with him,
incites a fury of protest. His comrades in the Communist
Party in particular criticize him for portraying such a
negative image of a black man. Be that as it may, Wright
had achieved his goal: to expose the reality of American
society, to express through Bigger Thomas's character
what you would later describe as "fury" and "hatred", as
a challenge to an America deaf to the demands of blacks.

Wright criticizes the American army head on, con-
demning their racism against blacks. He refuses to serve
during the war because, as he underscores in a letter to
one of his friends, "they ask us to die for a freedom that
we have never known." One of Wright's biographers,
Hazel Rowley, tells of how, in 1947, the writer distances

himself from America, as do most of his black counter-
parts. Wright is encouraged by Jean-Paul Sartre, Simone
de Beauvoir, Claude Lévi-Strauss, and, in the end, settles
in the City of Light with his wife—a Jewish American
woman.[37]

It would be an understatement to say that your admiration for Wright's journey knows no bounds. You have
read and re-read *Native Son* to the point that is serves as
inspiration for the title of your collection of essays, *Notes
of a Native Son.* You dream of being like him because
he had overcome the prevailing fatalism of his surround-
ings: "I had identified with him long before we met: [. . .]
his example had helped me to survive. He was black, he
was young, he had come out of the Mississippi night-
mare and the Chicago slums, and he was a writer. He
proved it could be done—proved it to me and gave me
an arm against all those others who assured me it could
not be done."[38]

You want to meet him, talk with him; learn from your
elder the meaning behind the effort, the discipline, and
the demands of writing. And, while you are at it, how to
achieve the same success.

Around this time, you knock on the door to his house
in Brooklyn. The writer welcomes you with open arms,
much to your great surprise, you who expected to find
yourself face to face with an emotionally distant author,
walled off by his fame. You are impressed, intimidated.

He puts you at ease. And while you are enjoying some bourbon, you announce, in the euphoria of the conversation, that you have written fifty or sixty pages, a novel entitled *In My Father's House*—which will become *Go Tell It On the Mountain.* You cannot gauge the level of excitement you have just stirred up in the mentor. He encourages you, and expresses a desire to read the pages that you had not brought with you. Do they exist, or had you made them up?

Leeming reports: "After a few days of furious writing, Baldwin sent the sixty pages to Brooklyn. Within a week Wright had read the manuscript, reacted positively to it, and, by way of Edward Aswell, his editor at Harper & Brothers, had recommended Baldwin for a Eugene F. Saxton Foundation Fellowship . . ."[39]

In 1945, you receive the fellowship of five hundred dollars in order to finish the book. It is a major step forward. And because the same prestigious Harper publishing house that publishes Wright supplies the funds, he speaks of you to his editor. A reading panel reviews your work. It is judged to be unpublishable, and, in the end, rejected both by that publisher and by Doubleday: ". . . when I was about twenty-one I had enough done of a novel to get a Saxton Fellowship. When I was twenty-two the fellowship was over, the novel turned out to be unsalable, and I started waiting on tables in a Village restaurant . . ."[40]

It is of course a painful disappointment, but you do not give up trying to emulate your mentor. You ask yourself what, in the end, makes *Native Son* have such a profound effect? Is it the shock of a white woman's murder by a black man?

You begin writing a new work, *Ignorant Armies,* which, as in Wright's book, tells a tale of murder with the issue of race at the heart of it: Wayne Lonergan, a bisexual, kills his rich wife for reasons related to their sexual problems. The voice of the narrative is unclear: although the story does gather its strength and truth from your life in Greenwich Village, marked by the "problem" of a sexuality that was more and more turned toward men, you speak in the place of your characters. What is more, this book contained two novels in one! The proof? Out of this "rough draft," two of your most well-known works of fiction would emerge: *Giovanni's Room* and *Another Country,* two novels that portray sexuality, even homosexuality, in the most tragic light.[41]

Following in your mentor's footsteps is not your only source of inspiration for the "failure," *Ignorant Armies.* Your own existence prior to your arrival in France is its own series of tragedies. As James Campbell relates to us about your life: "His father, crippled with madness, had died in a psychiatric ward. Baldwin had lost his Christian faith, which had plunged him deep into crisis, and helped him, one could say, accept the awakenings of his homosexuality—something very little accepted in Harlem, where he lived, and accepted even less in Church, where he had been preaching as a young minister."[42]

* * *

In New York you continue all the while to have meetings with your mentor. He takes off for Paris in 1946.

France will be the stage for your confrontation. Wright is as yet unaware that the pupil who had knocked on his front door had grown up, and, to survive, would need to trace his own path. Everything can perhaps be summed up with terrifying clarity in the following words: "His work was a road-block in my road, the sphinx, really, whose riddles I had to answer before I could become myself. [. . .] Richard was hurt because I had not given him credit for any human feelings or failings. And indeed I had not, he had never really been a human being for me, he had been an idol. And idols are created in order to be destroyed."[43]

4.

the destruction of idols:
from *Uncle Tom's Cabin* to
Native Son

In 1948 your friends George Salamos and Hasa Benveniste, also living in France, prepare to launch the journal *Zero* and call upon you to submit an article. The directors of *Zero* do not suspect that the text you will submit will ring in the era of hostilities between you and Wright.

The title itself has an agenda: "Everybody's Protest Novel" (translated into French as "Une opposition complice").[44] The article is simultaneously published in the *Partisan Review*.

The article begins by attacking works of fiction of the time, which, in your opinion, favor moral stories over art. In the "protest novel," as you call it, the author is indignant and cries out against what is supposed to be an abomination: slavery, racism, and general injustice. You think that this outrage is insincere, nothing more than a showing off of emotions. And it is a known fact that good literature cannot be created on good intentions alone. A very famous novel will serve as your primary target: *Uncle Tom's Cabin.* In your childhood, you read this book several times. It moved you, touched you.

First published in 1851, the novel takes place in antebellum America. Mr. Selby, a prosperous plantation owner somewhere in Kentucky, prides himself in treating his slaves with a certain degree of charity. Alas, drowning in debt, Mr. and Mrs. Selby must resign themselves to selling two of their slaves: Tom, the "good" old slave, and a child, Harry. Upon meeting Uncle Tom, the young Evangeline St. Clare is touched by the goodness of this man of color, and begs her father to buy him. Is this the end of the tender-hearted slave's peregrinations? Already weary, he must endure another separation. The novel follows his odyssey with a blend of emotion, sentimentality, and, above all, a clear conscience.

You no longer look at this book in the same light as you did in your childhood. From this point on you consider it to be a "very bad novel," which you criticize for its "dishonesty," "sentimentality," and its "inability to feel."[45] *Uncle Tom's Cabin*, in your opinion the crown jewel of protest novels, nevertheless inspired other noteworthy writers, especially several of your African-American colleagues, as Amanda Claybaugh confirms: ". . . many African-American authors from the first part of the 20th century were tempted, at a certain point in their career, to rewrite *Uncle Tom's Cabin*."[46]

On the list of these epigones, parodists, and imitators, some of whom have more talent than others, is Richard Wright, who publishes *Uncle Tom's Children* in 1938. Later, in 1973, there is Amiri Baraka with *Uncle Tom's Cabin: Alternate Ending*. Closer to our era, Amanda Claybaugh also mentions *Beloved,* Toni Morrison's novel, published in 1987. Faced with this flood of protest novels born under the influence of *Uncle Tom's Cabin,* your judgment is harsh: "It is indeed considered the sign of a frivolity so intense as to approach decadence to suggest that these books are both badly written and wildly improbable. One is told to put first things first, the good of society coming before niceties of style of characterization. [. . .] [Protest novels] are fantasies, connecting nowhere with reality, sentimental; in exactly the same sense that such movies as *The Best Years of Our Lives* or the works of Mr. James M. Cain are fantasies."[47]

As Benoît Depardieu judiciously points out, "While African-American writers in days past had emphasized the social origins of black paranoia, such as Richard Wright drawing inspiration from the Chicago school, Baldwin tackles its psychological roots, holding blacks responsible in some part for their own paranoia."[48]

* * *

By leading a crusade against protest novels, you earn your admission into the literary arena and create a reputation for yourself of being a Young Turk.

It must be remembered that *Uncle Tom's Cabin*, marketed as one of the first works of anti-slavery fiction, sold more than 300,000 copies in less than two years. The work becomes the only American novel to sell more than a million copies, following closely behind sales of the Bible. Amanda Claybaugh underlines what a great feat this is; at the time, novels were something akin to "public property": passed from one hand to the next, borrowed from traveling libraries, read out loud to the whole family, meaning that for each copy of *Uncle Tom's Cabin*, there were at least five readers . . .[49]

What sparks the success of this novel? It arrives without a doubt at the right moment, at a time when an ever-growing feeling of guilt was clouding the collective memory of white Americans. Beecher Stowe had moreover written her novel in reaction to the Fugitive Slave Act of 1850, declaring the return of all runaway slaves. The reception of the book is such that its characters become representatives of a part of the nation that considers itself open, enamored with liberty. At last, the reassuring, redemptive conversation that condemns and criticizes an entire system is in the open. Even better, these attacks and charges against the slavery of blacks come from a white woman, she herself a descendant of slave-owners. Based on this, the hasty conclusion is drawn that *Uncle Tom's Cabin* inspired the anti-slavery movement, a notion reinforced when President Abraham Lincoln, who had just signed the Emancipation Proclamation, invites this illustrious writer to the White House . . ."[50]

Uncle Tom, the good Negro, enters into the imagination of American society: advertisers latch on. The book is not only a best seller in the United States; its effect reaches international heights, too. In France, for example, George Sand takes up her pen in 1852 to commend the talent of her American female colleague: "The life and death of a child, the life and death of a negro, herein lies the entire book. This negro and this child are two saints from heaven. The friendship that draws them together, the respect these two perfect beings express for one another; it is pure love that fuels the passion of this tragedy. I know not what genius other than saintliness could have imbued this affection and this situation with so sustained or so potent a charm. [. . .] Honor and respect to you, Mrs. Stowe. One day or another, your reward already written in the heavens will also be of this world."

George Sand may be conscious of the novel's weaknesses, also noted by certain critics, but she is moved by the "long dialogues, the carefully studied portraits" of this book that "mothers, young children and servants can read and understand, and that men, even the highly-placed, cannot disdain." Her generosity is in the end one of a fully satisfied reader: "If the best praise we can offer a writer is to love her, the most honest we can be with a book is to love its defects. [. . .] These defects only exist in relation to artistic conventions that have never been absolute."

Taking the opposite approach to George Sand, you highlight the fact that these so-called protest novels deprive themselves of the demands of truth, and drown the very essence of the novel in a sanctimonious discourse: "Finally, the aim of the protest novel becomes something very closely resembling the zeal of those alabaster missionaries to Africa to cover the nakedness of the natives, to hurry them into the pallid arms of Jesus and thence to slavery. The aim has now become to reduce all Americans to the compulsive, bloodless dimensions of a guy named Joe."[51]

Uncle Tom's Cabin is a "convenient" work for everyone, although its very creation should awaken the collective consciousness and should not sacrifice historical reality for emotion. The characters in *Uncle Tom's Cabin* wear masks which, when removed, expose the greatest deception. Uncle Tom, for example, represents the stereotype of the black man inherited from the American imagination: he is illiterate, has nappy hair, and his "phenomenal hardiness" always allows him to endure the vicissitudes of the life of a captive, and, in the end, to "triumph" over them. With regard to the other slaves—George, his wife Eliza and their son—the author cannot escape from platitudes. The son resembles down to the last detail the stereotype of a shoeshine boy. Eliza, for her part, is lighter-skinned. While George is darker-skinned, he nevertheless does not have especially "negroid features," which allows him to pass. When he "escapes from his master's house disguised as a Spanish gentleman, he can walk through town without arousing anything other than admiration."[52]

The academic Amanda Claybaugh, who seems to want to give this classic its due justice, regrets that the work has been wrongly condemned. To those who criticize its racism and sentimentality, Claybaugh would have them remember that Beecher Stowe was the first American to imagine the black slave as a Christ figure . . .[53]

*　*　*

Harsher still are the criticisms you launch against Wright's *Native Son* at the end of "Everyone's Protest Novel," and, later, in another article entitled "Many Thousands Gone,"[54] which would appear in the *Partisan Review* in 1951.

With pencil in hand, reading your work closely, Wright is convinced that you are trying by any means necessary to destroy his work, especially when you place *Uncle Tom's Cabin* and *Native Son* on the same plane. You criticize his character Bigger Thomas for harboring a blind hatred that drives him to rape, an obsessive fear that leads to murder: "Below the surface of this novel there lies, as it seems to me, a continuation, a complement of that monstrous legend it was written to destroy. Bigger is Uncle Tom's descendent, flesh of his flesh, so exactly opposite a portrait that, when the books are placed together, it seems that the contemporary Negro novelist and the dead New England woman are locked together in a deadly, timeless battle; the one uttering merciless exhortations, the other shouting curses."[55]

But what distances you from Wright even further is his view of black American society. You consider the characters of *Native Son* to be far removed from the truth of daily life; since they are untethered from reality, they are also separated from the common and painful life of the black American. For you, the setting and dialogues ring false: "It is remarkable that, though we follow him step by step from the tenement room to the death cell, we know as little about him when this journey is ended as we did when it began; and, what is more remarkable, we know almost as little about the social dynamic which we are to believe created him. Despite the details of slum life which we are given, I doubt anyone who has thought about it, disengaging himself from sentimentality, can accept this most essential premise of the novel for a moment."[56]

As a result, the judgment you later render on the novel as a whole in "Many Thousands Gone" condemns in veiled terms the author's will to gloss over the most essential point: "What this means for the novel is that a necessary dimension has been cut away; this dimension being the relationship that Negroes bear to one another, the depth of involvement and unspoken recognition of shared experience which creates a way of life. What the novel reflects— and at no point interprets—is the isolation of the Negro within his own group and the resulting fury of impatient scorn. It is this which creates its climate of anarchy and unmotivated and un-apprehended disaster . . ."[57]

* * *

Shortly after the publication of "Everybody's Protest Novel" in the journal *Zero,* you go to Brasserie Lipp, in Paris—Chester Himes is there—and you don't expect to find Wright. But you do find him there, appearing very grim. He rebukes you for your attitude. He accuses you of betraying him, and, by extension, of contributing not only to the destruction of his position as an established author, but also to the annihilation of African-American literature by stripping it of what it inherently possessed: protest.

An argument breaks out between the teacher and the pupil. Wright, who had taken care to place his copy of the journal *Zero* on the table, pursues:

"All literature is protest!"

The pupil has been set free:

"All literature may be protest . . . 'but not all protest is literature.'"[58]

You will later give an account of this scuffle in "Alas, Poor Richard," one of the essays in your collection entitled *Nobody Knows My Name.* Your conflict had also been widely publicized by critics and academics alike, who heightened it to the level of one of the great literary rivalries in the American literary world.

By reiterating your criticisms of Wright's work in your piece "Many Thousands Gone" in 1951, two years after your attack against him in *Zero,* you confirm in some people's minds the notion that you are doggedly fighting your mentor. The article is perceived as the final signature on the divorce papers. This time the text is longer, more detailed, and in it you dissect *Native Son,* elaborating again on the notion of the protest novel, to better tear it apart. Wright is presented as the spokesman for the "new black man," who would have the weighty task of engaging himself in the social struggle after "swallowing Marx whole," and becoming convinced that the goals of blacks and those of the proletariat were one and the same. However this mission seems difficult to undertake since, as you point out, writers "are not congressmen." The text displays astounding skill, since in it you assume, like a character in a novel, the role of a white man who evokes then defends the status of the black American, from outside of his own community.

Reading "Many Thousands Gone," it is clear that you not only insist on this difference of literary opinion, but that you identify yourself by it.

* * *

The heart of the problem, however, lay elsewhere. The pupil had acquired his independence and now demands the right to think differently from his mentor. He does not try to hide this desire: ". . . I wanted Richard to see me, not as the youth I had been when he met me, but as a man. I wanted to feel that he had accepted me, had accepted my right to my own vision, my right, as his equal, to disagree with him."[59]

To Wright's fury, you try to temper the injustice, the wave of criticism crashing down on him. Confronted by those who believe he is cut off from reality, who reproach him for conjuring up a Mississippi and a Chicago that blacks had never experienced, for knowing nothing about jazz, to say nothing of the Africans who call into question how "African" he really is, your criticism brings things back to some kind of order, explains things, and possibly

even contextualizes these ambiguous and shadowy subjects. Some of Wright's opponents went too far—much
too far—such as the African who, while listening to the
author speak, shouted, "I believe he thinks he's white!"

You conclude, in response:

"I did *not* think I had been away too long: but I could
not fail to begin, however unwillingly, to wonder about
the uses and hazards of expatriation. I did not think I
was white, either, or I did not *think* I thought so. But
the Africans might think I did, and who could blame
them? In their eyes, and in terms of my history, I could
scarcely be considered the purest or most dependable of
black men."[60]

It would be inaccurate to say that you did not display a desire to have a frank discussion with your former
mentor—a discussion that would open the path toward
reconciliation. But it was too late; he had passed away.

* * *

Beyond the controversy, reduced more often than not
to a mere rivalry between two prominent writers, the
writer's status is at the heart of these two critical texts.
Would it not be better to retain this from the dispute,
and this alone? Langston Hughes, who reviewed *Notes
of a Native Son* in the pages of the *New York Times,*
compares the essayist and the novelist: "I much prefer

'Notes of a Native Son' to his novel, *Go Tell It on the Mountain* . . . In his essays, words and material suit each other. The thought becomes poetry, and the poetry illuminates the thought."[61]

One might ask how these subtle analyses on writing, the perception of history, or on the condition of blacks and the related themes that you develop in "Everybody's Protest Novel"—along with that of sexuality, themes that would become recurrent in your work over time—how all of that was relegated to the background behind your conflict with Wright. James Campbell is correct in affirming that "Everybody's Protest Novel" is "a piece of remarkable literature" that confirms the maturity of your style.[62]

* * *

The protest in question, the one you rally against, is in some ways reminiscent of the literary production from black, French-speaking Africa in the colonial and post-colonial periods. Several of these books—not necessarily written by Africans, but also by western writers discovering the "tropics"—fall back on some of the same sentimentality that can be found in *Uncle Tom's Cabin*.

At the very least they resemble each other in their desire to speak out against colonial atrocities or the treatment of blacks under colonial rule. In this case it is not the writer's implication "in the tropics" that is at stake, but rather his vision of his own society. The emotion the author infuses into his work more or less ruins any chance of achieving the objectivity and distance necessary for real intellectual work.

However there still exists this other danger, specific to the black writer: he is expected to put the "black issue" at the center of his work, expected to crowd his pages with characters of color, to adopt a confrontational tone, with the white man as his sole target. These unspoken watchwords are used to prompt African authors—especially the acolytes of negritude—to praise black civilization through frenzied incantations, or to rebel at the eleventh hour against the colonizers, or imperialism in general. And so this literature appears to be a vast campaign against the colonial system, counterbalanced by praise of African roots. But this criticism of the colonial system always results in predictable fiction: a backdrop of cities divided between whites and natives, and a message of bitter condemnation of Christianity and western civilization. Europeans, only, are responsible for Africa's sorrows.

Guinean novelist Camara Laye, for example, gets caught in the crosshairs of the self-righteous who saw his portrait of a "different Africa," a happier, more intimate, more personal Africa, such as the one that emerges in his masterpiece, *African Child*,[63] as a mark of carelessness and irresponsibility at a time when the known enemy was the colonial system. Countless authors would go down the anti-colonial path, as illustrated in the first works of Cameroonian Eza Boto, better known by the name Mongo Beti.[64] This man, like you, Jimmy, lived for a long time in France. He was known for his rebel spirit, his intellectual courage, and his willfulness. He believed that a writer should stand up, place blame where it is due and roar in the face of current events, and should not adopt "the sterile attitude of a spectator," to borrow from Aimé Césaire.[65] Considering it inconceivable to write during the colonial period about a young, African man, happy amongst his loved ones, he openly attacks his colleague Camara Laye with the following words: "Laye stubbornly closes his eyes to the most critical realities in his novel *African Child*. Did this Guinean not see anything other than a peaceful, beautiful, maternal Africa? Is it possible that Laye was not witness a single time to any atrocity of the French colonial administration?"[66]

* * *

I hold in high esteem the independence of the writer, Jimmy, and am weary of "herd-mentality literature." A writer should always share his own vision of the human condition, even if it runs counter to commonly held, moralizing beliefs.

A variety of African literature known as "child soldier" literature—or as "Rwandan genocide" literature, when it was created more in protest than in an effort to truly understand the tragedies—convinced me definitively that we were not yet free of the vortex of *Uncle Tom's Cabin,* and that the sentimentality and moralizing current that runs through some of these works does harm to African literature. If we are not careful, an African author will be able to do nothing but await the next disaster on his continent before starting a book in which he will spend more time denouncing than writing.

People will loudly remind me of our duty to be politically engaged, to tell the tale of Africa's woes, to publicly accuse those who drag the continent downward. But what is the value of political engagement if it leads to the destruction of the individual? Many hide behind this mask in order to teach us lessons, to impose upon us a vision of the world where there would be the true children of Africa on one side, and, on the other, the ingrates—meaning the latter are considered Europe's lackeys. By nature I distrust those who brandish banners; they are the same people who clamor for "authenticity," the very thing that submerged the African continent in tragedy.

In the introduction to her anthology of works from black Africa, the academic Lilyan Kesteloot pointed out "it is in fact preferable to confine oneself to the little

world of *me* than to make a great deal about negro una-
nimity without believing in it . . . The issue of political
engagement is decided in the conscience of each individual, and is not an aesthetic criteria . . ."[67]

Protest, if we broaden its meaning to include political
engagement, should transform the outcry, the emotion
and the exacerbation, into a timeless, creative act. In
this very way, Césaire's *Notebook of a Return to the Native
Land* will never age a single day. Conversely, I have only
to open certain works from the negritude era to notice
that they have not withstood the test of time. And if
their wrinkles are deep, it is because their authors forgot
that protest for protest's sake will never be a creative act,
but only a short-lived bleating. Protest—oh, pardon
me, political engagement—must simultaneously gather
strength from personal experience and communal destiny. Art cannot escape from being bound by violence.
And this is the bond, Jimmy, that extends from the
beginnings of your work to the end, as the Cameroonian
Simon Njami would illustrate in a biography he would
dedicate to you.[68]

5.

black, bastard, gay and
a writer

You brushed off labels like "Negro," "ghetto boy," "bastard," and, more than anything, "faggot."

If James Campbell, in his biography of you, fights against the latter label in particular—an easy insult for most of your adversaries—it is because he is aware that your homosexuality for you is the expression of your freedom, a way of being yourself, and not the expression of some deviation or, in his terms, of some "genetic ambivalence," definitions that distort the understanding of any individual.[69]

In your day, the contradiction was obvious: on the one hand, your country held up individual freedom to the level of a democratic ideal, but, on the other, sanctioned racial segregation. Consequently, as Dwight A. McBride attests, the ideological confrontation between capitalist and communist factions would alter the discourse on sex, race and the African-American community.[70] You would have a voice in this discourse . . .

In fact, after welcoming your article "Everybody's Protest Novel" into its first edition, the journal *Zero* published another of your articles in the following issue, entitled "Preservation of Innocence."[71] It is a brief text with philosophical leanings that revolves around the notions of normality and abnormality in human nature. The saga of the homosexual, according to your analysis, is that he must always confront the most profound grief: that he is abnormal because he has opted to turn himself away from his original function, that of a procreator, for a relationship bound to sterility. Since homosexuality is as old as the human race, the most suitable attitude would be to consider it as a material component of normality. Sex, with its myths, confronts us with the complexity of our behaviors and our beliefs. You remind us that men and women have imperfection in common, and are indivisible. Because of this, tampering with the nature of one has an impact on the nature of the other. Their absolute separation—man having to comfort himself in his masculinity, and woman assuring her own function as a woman—would destroy each of their souls. Although it is often repeated that women are more gentle, legends insinuate that they may be "mythically and even historically, treacherous."[72] Novels, poetry, theater, and fables have sometimes entertained this paradox, which only personal experience is capable of first clarifying, then blocking you in your tracks. "This is a paradox which experience alone is able to illuminate and this experience is not communicable in any language that we know. The recognition of this complexity is the signal of maturity; it marks the death of the child and the birth of the man."[73]

"Preservation of Innocence" remains the very first text in which you speak explicitly about homosexuality, before continuing to explore this theme in your following works, most notably in your second novel, *Giovanni's Room*.

In January 1985, two years before your death, you publish another article, "Freaks and the American Ideal of Manhood,"[74] in the famous erotic American magazine, *Playboy*, founded in 1953 by Hugh Hefner. This monthly periodical welcomes writers from time to time; the world's leading writers have published here, including Vladimir Nabokov, Ian Fleming, and Margaret Atwood.

In "Freaks and the American Ideal of Manhood," you examine the notion of masculinity by drawing on a multitude of autobiographical elements. You look at your own experience as a homosexual and try to understand the malicious gaze of the other, in particular the American heterosexual male.

Starting with the idea of androgyny, you argue that there is a woman in every man, and vice versa. As a consequence, ". . . love between a man and a woman, or love between any two human beings, would not be possible did we not have available to us the spiritual resources of both sexes."[75] However the American sexual ideal is intimately related to a certain idea of masculinity. It is this ideal that creates, among other things, ". . . cowboys and Indians, good guys and bad guys, punks and studs, tough guys and softies, butch and faggot, black and white."[76] The young, American man will therefore develop within this imaginary complex . . .

Your first homosexual experiences—even if they are then limited to a few encounters—take place in the bars of Greenwich Village. New York City at the time, according to McBride, attracts men and women who are exploring and expressing their sexual difference. In Greenwich Village, you and several other "faggots"[77] endure the jibes of the "moral police": "There were only about three of us, if I remember correctly, when I first hit those streets, and I was the youngest, the most visible, and the most vulnerable."[78]

At the age of sixteen these bad guys chase you, often under the amused and complicit watch of policemen. This makes you say that it was not the police you feared, but rather the guys who decided that you tarnished the respectability of the neighborhood.

Seek shelter? Where? In a movie theater? There you had to fear the wandering hand of an older man, or another man who, standing in front of a display of pornographic magazines, looks at you with eyes that say everything: "There were all kinds of men, mostly young and, in those days, almost exclusively white."[79]

Richard Wright would never see eye to eye with you about your lifestyle. Homosexuality for him was linked to perversion. He does not shy away from generalizations, since he remarks to one of his friends, when talking about you, "It's always the same thing with these homos" or, again, "Sure he can write, but he's a faggot."[80]

✳ ✳ ✳

The publication of *Giovanni's Room* in 1953 is quite an event. There are three reasons for this: the novel does not take place in America, there are no black characters, and the homosexuality of the hero is clearly stated.

France is the backdrop for *Giovanni's Room*, not without reason. This spatial displacement reveals your thirst for freedom, your desire for openness and to break with the protest novel. Your main character breaks free from the archetype of the African-American novel: David is not black. He resembles nothing of John Grimes, your "double" in *Go Tell It On the Mountain,* considered at the time to be one of the first books about the black condition.

David frequents the homosexual milieu in Paris while his fiancée, white and American, is traveling in Spain. The novel takes a unique look at the quest for sexual identity, in this way building upon reflections made in "The Preservation of Innocence" and that you pursue, near the twilight of your life, in "Freaks and the American Ideal of Manhood."

On the back cover of the first paperback edition we get a glimpse of the media buzz.

The *New York Herald Tribune* celebrates "the story of a young American man grappling simultaneously with the love of a man and a woman," before adding that , "Mr. Baldwin navigates these issues with an exceptional degree of candor, and yet, with such dignity and intensity that he avoids the trap of sensationalism." The *Evening Standard*, for their part, is even more won over: "Probably the best and certainly the most frank novel about homosexuality in years . . ."

The story is heart wrenching, as much for the characters' anguish as for the beauty of the writing, rendered lively and sensual through its poetic intensity and the strength of its imagery. Rather than mulling over the collective unrest over the black condition, you explore individual desperation, the hopeless tragedy of a man confronted with solitude and accepting a fate that drives him to self-destruction. In this lies the meaning behind the entire body of your work; understanding the collective through the individual.

Giovanni's Room nevertheless unleashed some very negative reactions in the black American community. The Black Panther activist, Eldridge Cleaver, does not mince his words and rejects in passing your entire body of work: "There is in the work of James Baldwin the most agonizing, complete hatred for Blacks, in particular for himself, and the most shameful, ardent and servile attraction to Whites than can be found in the work of any other black American writer of our day."[81]

Is this to say that the novel is deaf to the cries of the oppressed, impervious to the power of protest? In a few lines—no doubt quickly forgotten by your opponents—you give a reading of history distanced from the clash of civilizations, with all of the pain, bitterness, humiliation and rape it entails. At base it is a cry for reconciliation, for forgiveness and for redemption that we hear in the character David's confession on the first page: "My face is like a face you have seen many times. My ancestors conquered a continent, pushing across death-laden plains, until they came to an ocean which faced away from Europe into a darker past."

       ❖ ❖ ❖

Another Country, published in 1962, points to the source, beyond racial and gender divisions, of what divides an American society that clings to maintaining its puritanical appearances. This is a book that arouses once again the wrath not only of the black community, but also of prudish critics. When he reviews the novel for the *New York Times*, Paul Goodman issues the verdict of a cantankerous schoolteacher: "It is mediocre. [. . .] he [Baldwin] must write something more poetic and surprising."[82]

Paul Goodman is bewildered by the analytic approach of the characters and by the stark portrayal of racial prejudice. Goodman expects a sentimental novel that will reassure him, that will conform to the understanding he has of black American literature. Where this critic searches for something more surprising and poetic, you offer the raw reality of male-female relations, even relations where ambiguity and sexual confusion are deliberately displayed.

The first part of the book brings together a black male musician at the brink of total destruction, and Leona, a white woman he is supposed to humiliate by making love to her: "Here the act of sex is nothing more than the realization of a fantasy in which the black man has been implicated by the white man. Rufus falls psychologically and ends up committing suicide because he agrees to play the role that the white man had assigned to him in his imagination."[83]

Behind the sexual act you describe, the history of America is at stake.

"And [Leona] carried him, as the sea will carry a boat . . . They murmured and sobbed on this journey [. . .] Each labored to reach a harbor [. . .] He wanted her to remember him the longest day she lived. And, shortly, nothing could have stopped him, not the white God himself nor a lynch mob arriving on wings. Under his breath he cursed the milk-white bitch and groaned and rode his weapon between her thighs."[84]

With virtuosic skill, you distill in this heartbreaking sexual act all of the expected elements of the African-American experience: a crossing by boat, the predictable lynching of a black man for having approached a white woman, the revenge of a black man exacted on a white woman who has strayed from her area of control.

But when Rufus asks Leona what she is doing in the middle of Harlem, in a nightclub teeming with people of color, she responds most naturally:

"[Black people] didn't never worry me none. People's just people as far as I'm concerned."

How do you hold on to a love like that when you have to endure the glances of others? Can a sexual act that occurs in the darkness and intimacy of a shabby room in Harlem bond together two beings, unite them the following day, when they are faced with gossip?

There are no easy battles: "They encountered the big world when they went out into the Sunday streets. [. . .]

and Rufus realized that he had not thought at all about this world and its power to hate and destroy."[85]

For Goodman, there is nothing surprising or poetic in this, nothing, despite the disorder and the internal conflict of the characters who are haunted by this sexual experience, no—all of that passes unnoticed by our critic.

6.

between the black American and
the African: misunderstanding

In France, you hope to make progress on your quest for self-discovery, far away from the limitations imposed on you by your own country. Such a search proves to be more complicated than you imagined. The experience of migration places you face to face with other cultures, other people, and leads you to reconsider your ideas. Leeming writes that, ironically, once settled in Europe, you are forced to admit that the "old" continent had not in any way changed your heritage, and that the transformation would never occur: you would remain a black man as you had been in New York. Europe helps you, at best, understand what it means to be a black man. The Harlem ghetto had aroused in you a ". . . sense of congestion, rather like the insistent, maddening, claustrophobic pounding in the skull that comes from trying to breathe in a very small room with all the windows shut."[87]

Does an end to this confinement affect not only your body, but also your soul? Does Europe provide you with enough room to breathe?

After systematic rejection in your own country, you have to brave at present another reality—withdrawing into yourself, even watching yourself disappear: "The American Negro in Paris is forced at last to exercise an undemocratic discrimination rarely practiced by Americans, that of judging his people, duck by duck, and distinguishing them one from another. Through this deliberate isolation, through lack of numbers, and above all through his own overwhelming need to be, as it were, forgotten, the American Negro in Paris is very nearly the invisible man."[88]

Such invisibility allows you initially to be just a "man among others," no longer someone to be pointed at. This attempt to disappear is almost instinctive, as if you had to distrust the sudden freedom in a world that was yours to discover. However, and you learn this quickly, too, men of color are not all in the same boat in Europe: you are not treated the same as a black American as you would be if you were a black man from Africa, especially from the former colonies. History, you insist, disrupts countries and continents. And what greater site of disruption is there than Europe? Of course you need only to walk a few steps in Paris to assess the wealth and prestige of the French culture through its architecture, museums and the thoroughfares throbbing with tourists. Still, behind the thoroughfare, there is always a dark alleyway, a dead end, a cul-de-sac. And at the end of this alley, a man is seated on a bench, a can of beer in his hand—the other face of France is now forming: "alien" France, the France of refugees, exiles, and the formerly colonized. The pariahs of the Republic, in some sense. Among them are some who fought for France in the war and who wait in vain for their pension, or those whose relatives were killed at the front and hope to one day see the names of their family members in French history textbooks.

Their presence? Very visible. Like flies in a bowl of milk. And in their voices, a whisper of desperation.

Paris in this way becomes for you a true laboratory, playing ". . . a defining role in the elaboration of the 'African experience,' in the formulation and reformulation of a global blackness."[89] However the serious error regarding the perception of black communities in France, as Dominic Thomas points out in his essay, *Black France*, is to underestimate the different forces behind their emergence. One must be warned, he insists, against perceiving them as a homogenous community. This is how, in a novel like *The Black Docker*, from Senegalese writer Ousmane Sembène, the author can describe a black community in which the West Indian ranks higher than the Senegalese, a term referring to all Africans, regardless of their country of origin, with everything that it implies about France's attitude toward people of color from the black continent . . .[90]

How many times during my long stay in France do you think, Jimmy, I was asked if I was Senegalese? The collective imagination crafted a stock character that we inherited from our participation in World Wars One and Two, fighting for the French. Answering these inquiries with the response that I was Congolese required the patience and precision of a school-teacher, to explain that there were two Congos, even though the borders between the former Zaire (today called the Democratic Republic of Congo) and my country (the Republic of Congo) were carved out by Europeans! Did I also need to inform them that my capital, Brazzaville, had been the capital of Free France during the Occupation? Infuriated, I often gave up and accepted whatever had been decided about me, a "Senegalese" man. With some perspective, I realize that I was unwittingly reenacting the experience of my relatives who, in the French army and in the minds of everyone, were known as "Senegalese Tirailleurs" and accepted it.

* * *

What place is there, then, for a black American in this "Tower of Babel"? Your quest proves to be greater than you anticipate, Jimmy, extending beyond your particular case as an American citizen of color. It now encompasses the behavior of other migrants, and their way of life, but above all else, it encompasses France's attitude toward this juxtaposition of people washed up on its shores, each with his own motive, each with his own past . . .

In Paris, the African students you meet live ". . . in groups together, in the same neighborhoods, in student hotels and under conditions which cannot fail to impress the American as almost unendurable."[91]

Far from being alienated from himself, an African man does not harbor the same fear of rootlessness as an American man of color, even though he has endured history's injustice, and, unlike an American man of color, has not, "all his life long, ached for acceptance in a culture which pronounced straight hair and white skin the only acceptable beauty."[92]

On the contrary, Africans have the self-confidence—perhaps even an exaggerated one—of coming from a continent of clearly defined borders, from a supposedly sovereign nation, which they dream deep in their hearts will be emancipated, unchained from the bonds of dependence on colonial power. In this respect, they share a common heritage with other immigrants whose lands are still under French control.

Black Americans, on the other hand, have to seek out their identity. The product of a historical rape and a ruinous voyage, they want to retrace the steps of the crossing that cast them out of their native continent, Africa, into the cotton fields where strains of gospel rang out between cracks of the whip and the barking of guard dogs. Americans cannot forget the desire to rebel, or the leg cut off after an escape attempt, or the ropes of the gallows. Nor do young girls forget the vicious Master's abuse of power that would produce an entire line of bastard children.

In America, as Frantz Fanon points out, "the negro struggles and is opposed. There are laws that disappear, piece by piece, from the Constitution. There are decrees that forbid certain types of discrimination. And rest assured those things did not come as gifts. There are battles, defeats, cease-fires, and victories."[93]

Black Americans ran aground in a land that was not their own—the New World. This land of refuge reduced them to a status so low that they do not participate in the decisions of this nevertheless multi-racial nation, dominated by whites with a heavy hand. With this in mind you declare, "It is entirely unacceptable that I should have no voice in the political affairs of my own country, for I am not a ward of America; I am one of the first Americans to arrive on these shores."[94]

In short, while Africans are naturally attached to Africa, black Americans for their part mythologize it, spin legends about it, dream of it as a promised land, as if it represented the ultimate and absolute freedom. They long to return to the birthplace of their ancestors. Their Africa is, as a result, a kind of "dreamland."

Meanwhile, Africans want to change their land, their "real countries," to reclaim from the colonizers the power to decide the fate of their own people, to put an end to the exploitation of the wealth of their natural resources. It is a fight for freedom, a struggle to regain territory. Africans want to drive out the colonizers; black Americans are fighting simply to be recognized as full citizens.

And yet, black Americans and Africans are strangers to one another. Africans have a clear idea of Africa which involves them regaining control of the fountainhead, a fountainhead from which they believe all of the lost children—the so-called blacks of the diaspora—will one day come back to drink. Blood is thicker than water, after all.

Black Americans do not have a clear idea of Africa, but they do have certain ideas of Africa that situate them on one side of an unbreachable gap between myth and reality. There is the myth of their ancestors, torn from the continent; the reality is the battle they fight for acknowledgement and identity in their new homeland.

*　　*　　*

The uneasiness between Africans and black Americans is even more apparent when it comes to intellectual debate.

From the 19th to the 22nd of September 1956, the first literary congress of black writers and artists convenes at the Sorbonne in Paris, under the initiative of Alioune Diop, founder of the journal *Présence Africaine*. You are enlisted to cover the event for *Preuves et Encounter,* and you watch closely the birth of the Negritude movement by Aimé Césaire, Léon Gontran Damas and Léopold Sédar Senghor. Instead of drawing you closer to Africa, this encounter heightens your feeling of confusion. You consider the congress to be a true disappointment. The representatives of the Negritude movement are disconnected from reality, and when they express themselves—in France, in the French language, the language of their colonizers—their approach to the issues at hand is biased, in the sense that it is Franco-French leaning, and drowns the fundamental questions in theoretical posturing.

Negritude remains a vague and empty notion that seems separate from you. Certain African intellectuals—such as Manthia Diawara—do not attempt to hide their reservations on the subject. Diawara is not convinced that having a mutual "white adversary" creates a shared culture. And when Senghor, in a poetic speech, praises Richard Wright's *Black Boy,* you realize that the Senegalese poet has not yet understood the scope of the total misunderstanding that characterizes relations between Africans and black Americans. Senghor's interpretation of *Black Boy* in fact underlines Richard Wright's African heritage. Yet what Richard Wright authored in truth was an American autobiography that one cannot comprehend outside of the context of his personal experience as a black man in America, and all of the struggle, repression, denial and displacement that entails. In reality, the African intellectuals' takeover of this 1956 congress demonstrates their desire to appropriate the personal experiences of black Americans into the concept of Negritude in order to give the latter the appearance of being more open, of having a broader base.[95] Your uneasiness with this surfaces when, three years after the congress, you would confide the following to the historian Harold Isaacs: "[Africans] hated America, were full of racial stories, held their attitudes largely on racial grounds. Politically, they knew very little about it. Whenever I was with an African, we would both be uneasy . . . The terms of our life were so different, we almost needed a dictionary to talk."[96]

7.

the years of fire

Your essay, "The Fire Next Time," is published in 1963.

This text calls into question the structure of American society, which is deaf to the claims of minorities. In the same year, President John Fitzgerald Kennedy is assassinated as he begins his re-election campaign. This tragedy is a major blow to the progress of civil rights. Kennedy was fighting against racial segregation that was still common in some states, despite the 1954 Supreme Court ruling that outlawed it. He offered his support to Martin Luther King, Jr., and had received the leaders of the Civil Rights Movement in the White House.

During this time, concerned about not participating in the fate of your country, you leave France temporarily.

You are not a simple spectator, and certainly not merely a witness to history. Your voice is now counted among those at the center of the black community. It is your duty, first as a citizen, but also as a writer, who is seen henceforth as the spokesman of the voiceless. You could have uttered as your own the potent words of Aimé Césaire upon returning to his own homeland:

"And behold here I am!"

"Once again this life hobbling before me, no, not this life—this death, this death without sense or pity, this death that falls pathetically short of greatness . . ."[97]

Published in the United States in January, *The Fire Next Time* immediately springs to the top of the bestseller list. Several months later, your rising star lands you on the cover of *Time* magazine. Your words are closely monitored, and, even before this time, the FBI had opened a file on you (the famous file 100146553). You are not unaware that the FBI is watching you. You discuss it with your friends and family, talking about it more and more, as you fear that one day you will fall victim to a conspiracy, and that your days will end in mystery, like Martin Luther King, Jr., or certain members of the Kennedy clan. The smallest of your movements and activities is carefully recorded, to the point of being ridiculous, if one remembers that national security is at stake. File 100146553, now consultable via Internet, contains for example details such as "The current residence of James

Baldwin, the negro writer and playwright, is unknown. He had a romantic visit with Paul Robeson at the Americana Hotel. We report that Baldwin could be a homosexual; everything leads us to believe that he is."

In 1963 you are racing against the clock.

You undertake a tour of the South, the heart of the "Negro Problem." During this trip you do not hesitate to return to church, this time to preach another way of loving your neighbor—through tolerance, and the recognition of minority rights. You push the envelope so far as to call upon Robert Kennedy to respond to the police brutality with which a peaceful civil rights protest met in Birmingham, Alabama. Robert Kennedy invites you to speak with him along with other leaders of the black community. Could it have been any other way?

It is finally in August of 1963 that the famous March on Washington occurs. We hear Martin Luther King's, Jr., unforgettable "I Have a Dream" speech.

Throughout the course of the march, you are in the crowd, not far from Marlon Brando.

* * *

With "The Fire Next Time" you pen the most profound, political, and literary text on the subject of black freedom, future and status in America. Despite the initial thundering applause, voices of discord ring out shortly thereafter. Anticipating the fury about to be unleashed against you, Sheldon Binn notes in his review of your essay, "What he has drawn will not sit well even with some whites who count themselves as friends of the Negro. But he has not written this book of two essays to please. [. . .] Thus he has written from a heart which has felt a unique kind of hurt and a brain which has desperately sought hope in the face of what often seems to be the merciless logic of despair."[98]

Because of the threatening tone of your essay, you are accused of stirring up tensions between both sides; furthermore, this book is seen as a partisan act, and your ideas are labeled as extremist. Albert Memmi, who would later write the preface to the French edition of your work, remains perplexed and wonders if you are not making the same demands that Black Muslims make but in more bellicose terms: doing away with whites to leave room for blacks. He asks, "Does Baldwin ask for anything else when he suggests, calmly and level-headedly, that America should cease to consider itself a white nation? Should we also admit after reading his book that we are more afraid than Baldwin himself?"[99]

It is not a question of you pitting yourself against what many call, as your father used to, the "white devil." You must defuse both sides, rethink integration: "What one would not like to see again is the consolidation of peoples on the basis of their color. [. . .] Color is not a human or personal reality; it is a political reality. But this is a distinction so extremely hard to make that the West has not been able to make it yet. And at the center of this dreadful storm, this vast confusion, stand the black people of this nation, who must now share the fate of a nation who has never accepted them, to which they were brought in chains."[100]

"The Fire Next Time" opens the doors to everyone who wishes to understand your definition—if indeed you make one—of the black American as compared to his white countryman. The roar rising from the pages, the upheaval sparked by your ideas, and the crackling of an approaching fire are omens of things to come.

America is no fool: it has heard your message. But can it follow your lead? Is the book you have just written for or against America? Is this a book for your brothers of color, or against them? These questions are reminiscent of those that arose after the publication of Fanon's *The Wretched of the Earth,* with the subtle difference that in his text, inhabitants of Martinique confront their colonizers. In order to encourage the latter to heed the book's message, and indeed so that they understand that Fanon's work is addressed to their brothers of color, Jean-Paul Sartre writes, "Europeans, open this book, and enter into it. After several steps into the darkness you will see strangers gathered around a fire. Approach them, and listen; they are discussing the fate in store for your shop counters, and for the men who guard them. They might see you, but they will continue to talk amongst themselves, without even so much as lowering their voices . . . In these shadows, from which the sun will rise again, you are the walking dead."[101]

By the same token, America can no longer remain blind to the racial issue when it produces writers like you. *The Fire Next Time* warns of the dangers of the situation, but assures that all is not lost, that it is possible to elude the prophesy delivered in this song written by a slave:

> *And God gave Noah the rainbow sign*
> *No more water, the fire next time . . .*

"The Fire Next Time" concludes with this scriptural prediction, from the very Bible that you know like the back of your hand.

And what if America did not listen? What would happen?

"Well, if this is so, one has no choice but to do all in one's power to change that fate, and at no matter what risk—eviction, imprisonment, torture, death."[102]

These declarations are not unlike those of Malcolm X, who advocates obtaining rights by "whatever means necessary." Herein lies the point of convergence that Albert Memmi points out in his introduction to your work.

* * *

In his time, your colleague W.E.B. Du Bois asserted that the problem of the twentieth century was one between whites and blacks. "The Fire Next Time" tempers this assertion by declaring that, ". . . the value placed on the color of the skin is always and everywhere and forever a delusion,"[103] though nevertheless the racial question remains vital in the United States, in these years of fire.

In *Blues for Mister Charlie*, you borrow from a racist news item that would have serious political reverberations. On August 28, 1955, Emmett Till, a black adolescent, is murdered. A month later, his murderers are acquitted in court after a sham trial; America is even more shocked that the criminals admit their evil deed as soon as they are released from custody. The hasty verdict legitimizes the battle for civil rights that has been waged for many years already. What murder could therefore better represent the state of race relations?

The fourteen-year-old Chicago native has come with his cousin to spend his vacation with his great-uncle in Money, Mississippi—home to William Faulkner, Tennessee Williams, and Elvis Presley, but also to a segregationist and Ku Klux Klan stronghold—Emmett Till is kidnapped in the middle of the night by Roy Bryant, a grocer, and his half brother, J.W. Milam. They beat Emmett to death before throwing his body, completely disfigured, into the Tallahatchie River, a heavy weight tied to his neck with a piece of barbed wire. A fisherman discovers the body several days later. Although the motives for the murder vary depending on the testimony—Roy Bryant's wife maintains for example that the adolescent may have been disrespectful and might have spoken indecent words—was the punishment"administered to the young black boy by the husband and brother-in-law proportionate to the alleged provocation? Regardless of the answer, the fact remains that a human being has been killed. There was a crime. The motives are clearly racist.

Disregarding the pressures put upon her by the authorities, the mother of the boy demands that his casket remain open during the ceremony, so that everyone can comprehend the barbaric nature of the act that killed him.

The outrage generated by this heinous crime sparks an investigation by Medgar Evers and Amzie Moore, two members of the National Association for the Advancement of Colored People. They disguise themselves as farmers, in order to obtain evidence that might shed light on the death of the child. Their research led to the discovery of other black people murdered in the area, also lynched, then thrown into the river.

Then there was the trial. One must, no matter what, have faith in the country's justice system.

The jury? Do not hold your breath: it is composed of

twelve white men. These men acquit Roy Bryant and J.W. Milam after deliberations lasting just under an hour. One member of the jury, no doubt happy with the outcome, confesses upon exiting that he and his colleagues had to take a good "soda break" in order to reach a deliberation time that would be passable in the court of public opinion.

The verdict spreads unrest throughout America. The whole world is watching. What image will the country project of itself at a time when the international political context is the Cold War, and totalitarianism and attacks on individual liberties are more often than not attributed to the Soviet bloc, the world's other superpower, who is now carefully eyeing Washington's response? In any event, the sluggishness and awkwardness of the American administration at the time are bitterly criticized. Yet again America preaches freedom, railing against countries the world over for their barbarianism, while unable to fight against the most flagrant civil rights abuses within its own borders.[104]

Blues for Mister Charlie uses these facts to set the scene for the murder of a young black musician, Richard, by a white grocery store owner, Lyle Britten.

Is this play inspired by anger, or written with a desire for revenge? To the contrary, you insert a brotherly message into the text through the character of the victim's father, a staunch defender of civil rights, and whose friendship with a liberal white man aims to head off any hasty judgment or generalizations.

You dedicate the book to the civil rights activist Medgar Evers, a native of Mississippi, murdered that year, in 1963, five months after the publication of "The Fire Next Time." This leader of the Civil Rights Movement fought tirelessly for the black cause. A patriot, too, he took part in the Normandy landings. The University of Mississippi, still segregated at this time, closed their doors to him all the same when he applied to study law there. Somewhat ironically, this same institution would be the first to admit a man of color, James Meredith, one year after the assassination of the black leader.

History will remember, too, that Medgar Evers was killed on June 12, 1963. Was the date inconsequential? No. Evers was assassinated several hours after President Kennedy's televised speech in which he expressed his support for the Civil Rights Movement.

Blues for Mister Charlie received mixed reviews. You are criticized, as with *The Fire Next Time,* for fueling hatred toward whites, even though the heavily criticized play advocates tolerance and integration. At the time of its publication, the critic Walter Meserve sharply attacks your work as a playwright: "[Baldwin tries to] use theatre as a pulpit for his ideas. Mainly his plays are thesis plays—talky, over-written and clichéd dialogue and some stereotypes, preachy and argumentative."[105]

8.

on black anti-Semitism

in Harlem, black anti-Semitism is a reality. You decide to talk about it. The exercise is all the more delicate since by simply bringing up the topic you risk it flying back in your face like a boomerang. In his time, Karl Marx had been accused of anti-Semitism by his former teacher, Bruno Bauer, who had already drawn fire from all sides for having responded to the Jewish Question. Marx took up Bauer's argument and asked whether they should be freed as a group before the general population. Although Bauer asserts with good reason that "we must free ourselves before freeing others," Marx wonders to what extent freedom is possible in states that recognize the Declaration of the Rights of Man, but protect the idea of private ownership that allows owners to take advantage of their possessions in the most absolute way and, through such a power, to institute a system of exploitation to the detriment of society's most destitute.

This is, with few exceptions, the subject of a controversial article you publish in the *New York Times* in 1967: "Negroes are Anti-Semitic Because They're Anti-White."

Is this article a re-writing of *The Jewish Question* by Bauer, adapted to the American context? In any case, you start with an observation: in Harlem, it is an understatement to say that you hate your landlords. Anti-Semitism might be motivated more by the miserable conditions in which black Americans live than by blind hatred toward a part of the population who may or may not control everything. In this ambivalent relationship between Jews and people of color, there is something of a game of mirrors that dates back to the time of black slavery. The suffering and persecution of Jesus is systematically compared to that of the slave at the hands of his master. But, in other respects, a black man borrows from Jewish history, takes it as his own almost to the last detail, and, because of this, ". . . identifies himself almost wholly with the Jew. The more devout Negro considers that he *is* a Jew, in bondage to a hard taskmaster and waiting for a Moses to lead him out of Egypt."[106]

From where does this feeling of shared identity come? From the Bible, you assure us, since these "beliefs" from

the Old Testament are of Jewish origin. In a reversal of
roles, the term "Jew" would be used by blacks in Harlem
to label "all infidels of white skin who have failed to
accept the Savior" and who are responsible for the death
of Christ.[107]

This anti-Semitism is driven by more serious and
subtle motives: the black man blames the Jewish man
for "having become an American white man" who
profits from this status that pulls him out of the "house
of bondage" from which colored Americans struggle to
escape, despite the fact that they "were there before, and
for four hundred years . . ." Jews want the black community to understand the suffering they have known, the
acts perpetrated against them throughout history, and
even in their daily lives. In the absolute, Jews and blacks
share a common experience of suffering and rejection,
the tradition of wandering, and the search for a homeland. But therein lies, in your opinion, the great misunderstanding between them: "The Jew does not realize
that the credential he offers, the fact that he has been
despised and slaughtered, does not increase the Negro's
understanding. It increases the Negro's rage. For it is not
here and not now, that the Jew is being slaughtered, and
he is never despised here as the Negro is, *because* he is an
American. The Jewish travail occurred across the sea and
America rescued him from the house of bondage. But
America *is* the house of bondage for the Negro, and no

country can rescue him. What happens to the Negro here happens to him *because* he is an American."[108]

The example you draw on to support this argument is that of an African living in the United States. If the latter were a victim of some injustice, or of police brutality, he at least has recourse to the embassy of his native country, which will ensure his protection. An African has a country; he has a nation behind him. On the other hand, a black American who is wrongly imprisoned will find himself at a loss, will "find it nearly impossible to bring his case to court. And this means that *because* he is a native of this country . . . he has no recourse and no place to go, either within the country or without. He is a pariah in his own country and a stranger in the world."[109]

Jewish people, you think, are not only considered Americans; they can rely on allies throughout the world. You deduce that it would not occur to anyone to suggest to Jewish people to be "nonviolent." When they fought for Israel, this act was saluted as heroic: "How can the Negro fail to suspect that the Jew is really saying that the Negro deserves his situation because he has not been heroic enough?"[110]

* * *

You had been trained to despise Jewish people. The exasperation builds when you think of your neighborhood

transformed into a slum: neglected apartment build-
ings, broken windows, peeling paint, sagging stair-
wells, faulty heating and cooling, and, needless to say,
an unending stream of roaches and rats in the apart-
ments. "When we were growing up in Harlem, our
demoralizing series of landlords were Jewish, and we
hated them. We hated them because they were terrible
landlords, and did not take care of the building . . . We
knew that the landlord treated us this way because we
were colored, and he knew that we could not move out.
[. . .] Not all . . . were cruel . . . but all of them were
exploiting us, and that was why we hated them."[111]

Such allegations suggest that you generalize black
anti-Semitism in Harlem—some are quick to accuse you
of this—despite the irony your article employs to expose
the roots of a hatred based on several misunderstand-
ings. You point out that those facing you are Americans
first and foremost, regardless of being Jewish. But can
the latter be dishonest businessmen? "Jews in Harlem
are small tradesmen, rent collectors, real estate agents,
and pawnbrokers; they operate in accordance with the
American business tradition of exploiting Negroes, and
they are therefore identified with oppression and are
hated for it."[112]

A latent animosity defines the power dynamic between
the two communities. Black hatred toward Jewish people
does not prevent them from playing a role, or from being

hypocritical, because they require the services offered by those they loathe: "I remember meeting no Negro in the years of my growing up, in my family or out of it, who would really ever trust a Jew, and few who did not, indeed, exhibit for the them the blackest contempt. On the other hand, this did not prevent their working for Jews . . ."[113]

When it came time to discuss the thorny issue of the arrival of Jews and blacks on American soil, your arguments were far from convincing to your audience. For example, during a discussion with Budd Schulberg, who is Jewish, you make assertions that appall him: "I would like to insert a parenthesis on this point . . . a dangerous parenthesis, but it will serve to clarify in some way the bitterness of the black American. Here it is: I was here before you. I mean to say, historically speaking. [. . .] Historically speaking, I have been here for four hundred years. Let's say that you stepped off the boat last Friday, and you didn't yet speak English; on Tuesday I will be working for you."[114]

Schulberg's shock is tremendous, and his scathing reply throws you somewhat:

"What you just said, 'I was here before you,' is a stupid Muslim argument."[115]

Schulberg in this way alludes to the theories of Black Muslims that are popular at the time with Elijah Muhammad (one of the founders of the Nation of Islam) and Malcolm X, who proclaim the supremacy of the black race, and who advocate fighting—by any means necessary—in the name of the Nation of Islam, which today is lead by Louis Farrakhan. The target of the fight is anyone known as the "white devil," and, because of this, their theories are accused of being racist. Schulberg persuades you that such assertions are the crutches of fanatics and those who would believe in the supremacy of one group over an other, and that the "Aryans, too, believed the same thing."

Pulling yourself together, you clear your thoughts and repeat that the theory of the "white devil" never interested you: "I don't have the feeling of ever having been even vaguely attracted to the theory of the white devil. It is certainly not I who will propagate the idea, or who will allow someone to spread the teachings to any of my children, nor to anyone who is dear to me. But it's something else that I'm trying to get at . . ."[116]

You are trying to dissect the notion that Jewish suffering is considered a part of the world's moral history. As whites, Jewish people can achieve hero status through the suffering they endured and their recollection of them—America is dedicated to a boundless admiration for the white hero—while blacks who would do the same thing would be accused of "native savagery." In short, America's love of the white hero would lead it to a categorical rejection of "bad niggers."[117] This is the distinction that you believe sparked black anti-Semitism in Harlem at the time. Currently, it is a distinction that still affects relations between various demographics in France, where the question of "competing for historical recognition" is being hotly debated.

You protest the silence of the Western press, for example, on the atrocities committed by Belgium during its colonization of Congo. Would we have needed to rebuke this silence had the tragedy occurred in the white world? Herein lies the responsibility that you place on the shoulders of the Christian world, since the acts of violence committed during the colonial period were accompanied by conversion of the conquered peoples: "And since the world at large knew virtually nothing concerning the suffering of this native, when he rose he was not hailed as a hero fighting for his land, but condemned as a savage, hungry for white flesh. The Christian world considered Belgium to be a civilized country; but there was not only no reason for the Congolese to feel that way about Belgium; there was no way that they could."[118]

* * *

Is there a disproportionate amount of outrage sparked by an event, a disproportion linked to a kind of hierarchy of communities? Let us examine a case that took place in France, in our adopted land: the death of young Ilan

Halimi in the Paris suburbs. The facts come together like the plot of a horror film. For several weeks, twenty-three-year-old Ilan Halimi is held captive by a gang from Bagneux, who torture him to death. Because he is Jewish. The French daily *Le Parisien* even reveals on the front page that inhabitants of this suburb were aware of the young man's confinement, but chose not to inform the authorities. The opening pages of Gabriel Garcia Marquez's *Chronicle of a Death Foretold* come to mind . . .

The political reaction is strong and unanimous in the face of this crime clearly motivated by anti-Semitism. The story shocks the entire country, especially as other incidents of anti-Semitic crimes had been reported several months earlier.

Can we see evidence in this of two different degrees of outrage? To be clear—and let's not beat around the bush about it—would the murder of a black man in France, under the same conditions, have generated the same widespread outrage?

Blacks in France undoubtedly remain unaware as yet of the "weapon" of outrage, an extension of Gandhi's position, a new form of nonviolent action. Outrage as I am using it, Jimmy, does not mean externalizing hatred, much less the zealotry deployed with the aim of quickly repairing an injustice "by any means necessary," but means rather exposing the incident through coherent and objective analysis. As a consequence, one community's ability to react to it will condition another community's interpretation of a tragedy. The greater the outrage of a community, the greater the repercussions will be on society as a whole, and, by extension, on political authorities.

However, it appears that black people in France, faced with an act of violence, first measure the extent of the outrage that a similar event perpetrated against another "community," that they believe to be protected and more supported by political authorities, would generate. From that perspective, they begin to draw conclusions, particularly that Jewish people control the system. It is clear that the death of Ilan Halimi feeds the anger of anyone who respects human life—in the same way that the death of Emmett Till in Mississippi does—because first and foremost we are talking about the obliteration of a man's life. The anti-Semitic motive—one could say *mutatis mutandis*, skin color, political convictions, etc.—adds to the exasperation, incomprehension, and the bewilderment. Ilan Halimi died because he was Jewish. He could also have died for being black, Muslim, or because he was a political opponent.

Still, in France, on March 25, 2006, several prominent French public figures, including Alain Finkielkraut, Jacques Julliard and Bernard Kouchner, added their names to an open letter against "anti-white hate crimes," a letter initiated by the Hachomer Hatzaïr Zionist movement and Radio Shalom, following high-school student demonstrations that had occurred in the country two weeks before: "Two years ago, almost to the day, on March 26th, 2003, several of us sounded the alarm. Four young people belonging to the Hachomer Hatzaïr movement had just been attacked, outside of a protest against the war in Iraq, because they were Jewish. An attempted lynching in the heart of Paris is a scandal. The efforts of the media, political figures and humble citizens were tremendous. But today high-school student demonstrations have become, for some, an opportunity for what might be called 'anti-white hate crimes.' High-school students, often alone, are thrown to the ground, beaten, robbed and assured by their attackers, with smiles on their faces, that it is because they are French. Let this serve as a renewed appeal because we will not accept this, and because for us, David, Kader and Sébastien have the same right to dignity as anyone else. Writing this type of letter is difficult because the victims have been appropriated by the far right. But that which goes without saying is, in fact, better said aloud: no group should be targeted, period. For us, it is a question of fairness. We have talked about David, and Kader, but who is talking about Sébastien?"[120]

Parallels between the United States are quickly drawn: during a press conference, one of the signatories of the letter, the philosopher Alain Finkielkraut, warns: "We are facing a Farrakhan-style battle."[121]

Could the black American leader of the Nation of Islam, Louis Farrakhan, influence people in France? I do not believe so, for the simple reason that the idea of a black community in France is a superficial one, and that the history of black Americans has roots which cannot be compared to the black presence in France. To make this comparison is to see every black person as a potential member of the Nation of Islam, in the way that black American Muslims understand it.

Long ago, blacks in France believed—and perhaps still believe—that having the same skin color meant speaking the same language, and facing the same direction. However, Africa is disparate, and divided. The culture of one African country is not necessarily that of another. Moreover, the displacement experienced by these countries, in addition to the displacements created by French colonial policies—including drawing colonial subjects into European wars—create personal histories deeper than any collective history of meeting in the "land of refuge." Education, political asylum, financial reasons and civil war on the black continent cannot give rise to a common history. These issues are neither specific to nor define the black race.

In some respects, I would say that the black community in France is an illusion, that it does not exist, for the plain and simple reason that the existence of a community is an intellectual and historical construct.

The existence of a so-called black community in France would presuppose a collective awareness of it, and I am referring to an awareness based on reasons beyond skin color, or belonging to the same continent, or to the more broadly defined black diaspora, which, more and more, proclaims its singularity, its "rhizomic identity," as Édouard Glissant would say.

It is through the present, through encounters, that this common identity is woven; sometimes we can even find ourselves surprised by how much it conflicts with the idea of a "primary root" that would lead us all back to a single past. This other awareness—that black Americans have been able to develop throughout their long and troubled history—this other awareness, as I was saying, should take into account the experience lived out on French soil. The effect outrage has as a response to an injustice depends on a collective cause, which is given greater value than the individual in an abstract sense, and is related to our humanity. In this way, when we are witness to an act of racism, when we witness an act of anti-Semitism, it is our sense of humanity that sustains injury.

* * *

Jimmy, citizens of black Africa are convinced that African-Americans today have succeeded in creating a community whose influence is so far-reaching that it affects the destiny of the entire United States. And so, when confronted with an attitude that is unjust, with an act of racism or discrimination, black Africans automatically ask themselves, "So what would our black American brothers have done in this exact situation?" Is it surprising then that certain observers are alarmed to see "racist," Black Muslim ideas imported into France?

Whatever the case may be, the comparison with the black American community is further corrupted by the fact that blacks in France do not have the same experience of migration, and that they do not have the same "score" to settle with France as black Americans do. On the other side of the Atlantic, racial segregation was institutionalized—France, on the other hand, played a significant role in "the elaboration of the 'African experience' in the formulation and reformulation of a global blackness,"[122] thanks to the diversity of the black migrations that it experienced and still continues to experience today.

Blacks in France can certainly draw inspiration from their American black brothers, and envy the rights they have achieved in the United-States—however, let us be reminded, with the help of Fanon, that every right was wrested from fierce struggle that ended with the United States painted into a corner. From these struggles great leaders were born and immortalized in contemporary American history. What these black leaders shared in common was that they refused to have their humanity called into question.

It is Fanon who emphatically highlights: "No, I do not have the right to come scream my hatred at the White man. I do not have a duty to murmur my gratitude to the White man . . . if the White man questions my humanity, I will show him, weighing down on his life with all my force as a man, that I am not the "Y'a bon Banania" that he insists on imagining . . ."[123]

9.

the ghost of
Saint-Paul-de-Vence

as the summer of '86 begins, the specter of death looms over Saint-Paul-de-Vence.

You withdraw to the back of a room, near an old fireplace; shut away from the world, you stretch yourself out on a mattress on the floor, pushing away the inexorable verdict with an authoritative hand, although the hand is weaker than in the days when your power as a civil rights activist and your finesse as an essayist made all of America tremble.

Until your last day, until your last breath, you hammer away at the keys of your typewriter, as if to engrave your final wishes, to write the sentence with which posterity would remember the name, that would perhaps utter nothing more: James Baldwin . . .

Unmoved by your work ethic and blind to beauty, Death comes to Saint-Paul-de-Vence in 1987. She spends no time contemplating the splendor of the ramparts, turns her back on the hills, the Mediterranean and the Esterel Massif. She arrives by way of the old village cemetery without slowing down, because this time she does not plan to miss you. Death knows you, but only from afar; perhaps she is unable to face your big eyes that would have studied her from head to toe.

If on that night you had gotten up, if you had gone to the window and opened it, you might have seen the bad omens: the awkward flight of lost passerines, the cawing of crows troubled by the blanket of black covering the sky for weeks. You might have noticed the passing shadows of the artists who earned Saint-Paul-de-Vence its reputation. Why do they linger in the famous hotel, Le Robinson, surprised that it is now called La Colombe d'Or? The walls of the Colombe d'Or are decorated with the paintings and drawings of Braque, Picasso and Matisse. Who could help but smile when hearing that it was with these that the artists paid the restaurant? No matter— these souls have wandered over to La Pergola and La Résidence. There again they discover a new name: Café de la Place. From your window you could have waved at these illustrious friends. Matisse, Chagall, Renoir, and Modigliani would have been the first to wave back to you. Then Cocteau and Prévert, followed closely by the film people, Cayette and Audiard. The latter would have called out to you, as a consolation against your imminent death, "The ideal thing, when one wants to be admired, is to be dead." And to make you laugh, he would have thrown in one of the sayings that made him famous: "The French irritate me immensely, but as I speak no other language, I am obliged to talk with them."

The musicians—I am thinking of Armstrong and Miles—would play a piece that would rouse the Provençal countryside. And yes, Bessie Smith's voice would be there, too. She would sing out in a clear voice a strain from "Back Water Blues." Once more you would be moved by this woman who sang about her despair, though she accepted it all the while.

In the background, hazily drawn on the scene, you would see Romy Schneider, Tony Curtis, and Roger Moore, while your friend Yves Montand and Lino Ventura would be arguing over a game of pétanque. You would remember the time when you discovered this fascinating region, and when you still lived in the Hôtel Le Hameau, several kilometers from the village, on the road to La Colle. You would think back to the face of your great friend Mary Painter who first spoke to you of Saint-Paul-de-Vence when you needed rest after a hospitalization.

In 1950 you meet Mary Painter in Paris, in a bar. She was working as an economist at the American Embassy. You never concealed your love for her, to the point of admitting that not being able to marry her meant that you would never marry any woman. In 1950, having already come to terms with your homosexuality, you knew that it was impossible for you to hope for a serious romantic relationship with a woman. And, as David Leeming points out, you did not want to live a lie, nor to find yourself in a situation like your character from *Giovanni's Room*, David, who, disturbed by his sexual problem, had to lie to his fiancée, Hella.

You nevertheless remained close to Mary Painter, in whose home on the rue Bonaparte you listened to Beethoven and Mahalia Jackson with your Swiss partner Lucien Happersberger, and smoked PX cigarettes.[124]

And so it happened that Mary Painter knew Saint-Paul-de-Vence from the time she had spent there with her husband.

After your stay at Le Hameau, you moved into a room at the large farm belonging to Jeanne Faure. Many people wondered how you managed to convince her to open the doors of her property to you. She was in fact very distrusting of people of color; it was a distrust that bordered on loathing. All of your biographers evoke the bitterness of this "pied-noir," who had lived in Algeria during the colonial period.[125] Uninformed and hurt, she had always believed that black people had helped chase the French out of Algeria, her homeland. You needed references from Simone Signoret, Yves Montand and the owner of the Colombe d'Or before you could sign the rental agreement. Later, when she would sell you a part of her home, she would deem it necessary to block the door leading to her rooms with an armoire, while at the same time alerting her neighbors to justify her behavior: "You never know what to expect from these 'nee-gers.'"[126]

Jeanne Faure is not the only one to harbor such feelings. The fear of a foreigner in a small village, who happens also to be a man of color, is not surprising. You receive by mail anonymous threats and insults. This does not discourage you; you have known nastier situations. All you have to do is talk with people. Your open spirit and your generosity break down the walls around you, little by little. You walk through the village, greet the passers-by, invite some of them for a drink in the local bar. You surprise many people with this simple approach.

In time, even your landlady becomes less suspicious of you. She invites you to dine with her, and is not offended that you return the favor. She enjoys listening to you talk about your America, your fight for the rights of your countrymen, and about what you are in the process of writing.

On the day of her brother's burial, you are spotted in the funeral procession. In suffering, the depth of man's spirit is discovered. From that moment on, the black man who smokes all day long charms Jeanne Faure, tapping away at his typewriter, and openly displays his good mood. Many people remark on your neighbor's presence when François Mitterrand awards you with the Legion of Honor in 1986. And when Jeanne Faure finally decides to leave the village, she sells you her entire property. A change of heart? Certainly. But Miss Faure also had financial troubles.

* * *

On your deathbed, you can do nothing more than imagine these famous figures. You are waging a war against your own shadow. Cancer gains ground. The treatments intensify and let you believe that hope and faith will take it away. Who would not believe it, after all, especially after the surgery on April 25, 1987, that allowed you to eat and work again? You devote yourself to writing a play, *The Welcome Table.*

The lull is short-lived. Your illness returns at a full gallop, and your loved ones draw near. Your partner Lucien Happersberger arrives from Switzerland. Your little brother, David, comes in from New York. Your personal secretary, Hassel, was also there, always faithful and devoted. Your neighbors surround you. They stop by, knock softly on your half-opened door, and David leads them to you. They come to see "Jimmy," a man who chose Saint-Paul-de-Vence as his home, as his place of freedom. They want to hear your laughter. Alas, it has all but disappeared, replaced instead by a fixed grin that is either the beginning of a smile or the glimpse of an inner pain you struggle to conceal.

And who are the neighbors? I think mostly of the musician Bobby Short. He lives not far from there, in Mougins. With Bobby at the piano you used to sing little songs with him; David, with his deep voice, summoned his memories and the repertoire of old songs you had composed, some when you were still just a schoolboy.

David helps you move from your bed to your worktable. Sometimes, in a fit of pride, you refuse his help, which you see as defeat. Sick, yes, but incapable—no. You dread leaving your bed just to have your brother lead you back to it like a child. The persistent David has the gentleness to remind you that you carried him on your back countless times in his childhood. Why should he not take his turn in carrying you?[127]

* * *

This sudden affection feeds your distress; distress at leaving behind a shroud of sadness, at not finishing your last sentence. The anguish of telling yourself that you will join the other world, and will have to talk with David Baldwin, your father. You will have to tell him how he was wrong to believe for so long that he was nothing but black trash, and wrong for not knowing that he was beautiful. Hassel, who is very superstitious, admits privately to having seen your shadow on the wall. And so the fatal moment has arrived. Hassel is convinced of it. However, he clings to the idea that he has always seen you cheat death, has always heard you insist that you would leave the earth in a spectacular way, not weakened by illness. Hassel is not unaware that you see Death, and that you are now talking with her. No, you do not want to negotiate your departure date from the world. You have accepted the idea of your death.

Hassel has many reasons to believe that you will survive the 1st of December 1987. But there is the shadow on the wall that grips him. Can one survive an omen? It is possible. After all, he thinks to himself, you are an exceptional being. Had you not survived two heart attacks? These warnings did not prevent you from attending to your business, honoring your engagements around the world, even though you had to reduce your consumption of tobacco and alcohol.

You have to live your life. For these reasons, while you are attending a performance of your play *The Amen Corner* at London's Tricycle Theater in February 1987, no one could have imagined that you had already reserved a hospital room in Nice for cancer surgery.

This time the doctors can do nothing more. The situation is desperate. Your entourage conceals from you their despair and the seriousness of your condition. But you are not so easily fooled. Your doctors assure you that you will make it through the end-of-year holidays without danger.

You begin to organize, therefore, a big event in Saint-Paul-de-Vence.

In these final hours when the world must seem very still, a woman appears before you, her face hidden by a dark veil. Your curiosity pushes you to remove the veil: it's her, your mother. Now she wipes her thick glasses, foggy from tears. Yes, Emma Berdis Jones is somewhere in this room, despite the thousands of miles that separate you. You call her often, and, from Harlem, she listens to you with the despair of a mother who has always known that her child was fragile, and yet predestined to carry the world on his shoulders.

Your conversations remain unchanging. She offers you advice as she did long ago, when you were a child in Harlem: take care of yourself, don't stay up too late, above all don't smoke too much, drink even less, don't give in to the taunts of those who attack you now that you are a public figure, or because your sexual orientation differs from theirs. For her, despite your international influence, you remain little Jimmy, who followed her around the house . . .

❊ ❊ ❊

At present your world is reduced to the four walls of your bedroom. The biographer James Campbell paints a striking picture of this room that holds the secret of your final hours: a room submerged in soothing darkness, but whose wall paintings create an atmosphere of hallucination.[128] In this confinement, as Campbell points out, there is the feeling that Simone Signoret and your other friends dead long ago have come to bring you news of the other world.

You still have the strength to give an interview in November 1987 to the writer and professor Quincy Troupe who will publish, two years after your death, a collection of essays dedicated to your memory.[129] In the mix are the voices of Toni Morrison, Amiri Baraka, Maya Angelou, William Styron, Chinua Achebe and Mary McCarthy, among others.

An abundance of project ideas fill your mind. You plan, for example, to write a long introduction for a publisher in London who will publish two paperback editions of Richard Wright's novels. A large number of critics and biographers would doubtless consider such a presentation as reconciliation between the mentor and the pupil. But you will not have time . . .[130]

In November 1987, you had planned to host a large dinner at your home for Thanksgiving. You imagine that there will be a lot of people there. You and your friends will dine outdoors, you will smoke, crack a few jokes.

Alas, you will not know this farewell filled with laughter and song.

You leave this world on December 1, 1987. After the inhabitants of Saint-Paul-de-Vence have said their good-byes, your body is brought back to the Harlem of your childhood. There is a viewing at the Episcopal cathedral Saint John the Divine. From your casket you can hear the sobs of cultural icons as well as those of strangers you managed to win over.

You are buried at Ferncliff Cemetery in Hartsdale, New York, on December 8, 1987.

10.

on the need to read or
reread you today

If you return to this world, Jimmy, you will judge your homeland even more severely than you did when you were alive. Inequalities are now more subtle, and more hidden, in a society which has not yet resolved the issue that had been so important to you: redefining American identity, or, in your words, addressing integration through the "power of love." Happily, Judgment Day is not yet upon us.

On the other hand, if you cast a fleeting glance toward France, our mutually adopted homeland, you will be shocked to discover that your words and writing are as relevant today as they ever were. France is still burdened with the skeleton in the closet—the country's "colonial activity"—a chapter of its history so controversial that a line has been drawn in the sand between those who would systematically lay claim to memory and the "competition for victimhood," and those who call for an end to the "tyranny of guilt," in keeping with the notions of Pascal Bruckner who, in 1983 evokes the "tears of the white man" and his "suspicious tears."[131] By way of introducing *The Tyranny of Guilt,* the French author and essayist asserts, "Strangely, we are experiencing today a one-way street of guilt: the latter feeling is demanded of only one group, ours, and never of other cultures, of other regimes who cloak themselves in their alleged purity to blame us more easily. But Europe accepts too willingly the blackmail of blame, if we are so taken with self-flagellation, and covering our head with ashes, is it not our secret wish to exit history, to shelter ourselves snugly in the cocoon of contrition, to discontinue action, to escape from our responsibilities? Repentance is perhaps nothing more than a triumph of the spirit of abdication . . ."

Later, in the preface to the paperback edition of the same book, Bruckner would reveal the difficulties he encountered upon publication of his article, proving, as if it were necessary, that this subject remains a very sensitive one in a French society that has little by little constructed itself on a vision that is, to say the least, simplistic: executioners on one side, victims on the other. Between the difficulty of interpreting the meaning of its history and the need to curb the volume of grievances against it—grievances that could certainly last for centuries—France is on the brink of an ideological split.

Setting aside any doubts one might express about some of Bruckner's theories—how for example, if asking these questions, can one not expect generalizations from the fiercest opponents, not only from the side of the "victims," but also from his own side that "cries," and now repents— one is obliged to respond to his outstretched arm and to his sense of dialogue: "There are no innocent or chosen people; there are only more or less democratic regimes capable of correcting their failures and of assuming responsibility for their past transgressions . . ."[132]

He argues against the "triumph of the abdication-minded," which is in conflict with the triumph of the accusation-minded from the other world that he considers to have been at all times and in all places the punching bag for the white man's monstrosities and appetite for conquest. Between these two antagonistic positions, the side that cries and the side that accuses, the cease-fire is a long way off. Self-criticism is a rare commodity we no longer find in the marketplace. Add to that the absence of thoughtful and objective reflection, and the coming together of people is further undermined, and the path down the famous "competition for victimhood" further widened.

In 1961, Jimmy, your friend Jean-Paul Sartre, in his preface to Frantz Fanon's *The Wretched of the Earth,* legitimized this theory of victimization: "Our victims see us in their injuries and in their chains: this is what renders their testimony indisputable. They need only show us what we have done to them to make us understand what we have done to ourselves. Is this useful? Yes, because Europe is in danger of dying."[133]

To the Europeans who insist that they cannot be held responsible for the consequences of colonization—because they were never in the colonies, you see!—Sartre underscores the duty of solidarity burned into their collective conscience, which is probably the cause of the tears currently being shed by the West: "These are your pioneers—you sent them overseas, they made you rich. You warned them; if they spilled too much blood, you would politely disavow them, in the same way a State—no matter which—maintains a network abroad of agitators, rabble-rousers and spies that it disowns when they are taken . . ."[134]

* * *

Meanwhile, Jimmy, the strict regulation of migration and the political restructuring of European states as one bloc have created "individuals without fixed nationality." The entire definition of the immigrant's status has to be revised. The presence of these people from former French territories becomes as a result the subject of great debate, and the subject of agitation and political posturing during election campaigns.

The African immigrant is no longer the same, to be sure, but one must from now on consider his descendants who, not being from "over there," must nevertheless find their place "here." They are torn between two, sometimes three continents—their place of birth does not guarantee them any sense of belonging—while at the same time the "values of the Republic" to which they must adhere do not take into consideration the history of their ancestors. The little "black grandsons of Vercingetorix" can do nothing but try to see themselves in Rimbaud's *Bad Blood:* "I have the whitish blue eye of my Gallic ancestors, the narrow skull, and the clumsiness in conflict. I find my clothing as barbaric as theirs. But I don't butter my hair. The Gauls were the most inept skinners of cattle and scorchers of earth of their time. From them I take: idolatry and love of sacrilege;—Oh! all the vices, anger, lust,—magnificent lust—above all lying and sloth."

The son of an immigrant could perhaps from one day to the next be picked up from school and deported with his parents. It is the politics of diversity that is being discussed now; you would be surprised to discover that a debate has begun to rage in France over affirmative action, and that your native country is sometimes used as a model to follow.

We are still a long way from understanding that *other* is not necessarily a synonym for loss and subtraction, and even less so of division, but rather of addition and even multiplication, two operations that we can no longer engage in sparingly in a world that challenges more than ever the rigid definition of national identity.

It is in this sense that the philosopher Achille Mbembe reproaches France for its lack of the kind of hospitality practiced mostly by the United States that has allowed it to "captivate and recycle the world's elite. Throughout the last quarter of the 20th century, [the United States'] universities and research institutions managed to attract nearly all of the top black intellectuals on the planet."

But can we applaud the American model of hospitality blindly, Jimmy? The Cameroonian philosopher argues, "Whether we like it or not, things now and moving toward the future are such that the specter of the third world in our culture and collective lifetime will not rise in a quiet way. The presence of this specter forces us to learn to live exposed to one another. And although we have means of limiting this increase in visibility, in the end, it is inevitable. Therefore we must, as quickly as possible, make the specter into a symbol that facilitates understanding."[135]

* * *

At the same time, relations between the "dark continent" and France bring to mind a children's story with, as yet, no moral. Europe and Africa avoid the issue of history—or at least stifle their differing views of it—while quietly muttering their respective reproaches behind each other's backs. They are like a couple who hides their incompatibility in public, promising to a family court judge, saddled with the same case for centuries, to keep their dirty laundry behind closed doors.

Is there any hope for these spouses? I am not sure, because when they run into each other on the street corner, they hastily gloss over their differences, telling each other they will discuss everything later. But one of them never comes home on time, returning whenever he feels like it, adding to the ever-growing list of infidelities while swearing, on all that is holy, his undying love.

To stick with fairy tales, Jimmy, I would say that once upon a time, a rooster crossed the ocean, ran aground on African shores, did without parental consent to force himself on the dove as her husband, accumulated acts of domestic violence, and all with such an arrogance that he practically declared war on any other animal eyeing his barnyard. This is how, in my country, Congo-Brazzaville, the Gallic rooster and the Belgian lion would have killed each other over a patch of land had it not been for the intervention of the German mediator who made them sit down at a table in Berlin to work out a way to share.

The marriage between the rooster and the dove lasted for decades. The 1960s were the divorce years, sometimes through mutual consent, but more often than not through the wife's bitter fight for liberation; the losses were incalculable and would deplete the inheritance of the children born of this union. The rooster decided the settlement. He would leave, but his spouse would be nothing more than a dependent at the mercy of his charity. The rooster could return to the marital home whenever he pleased, and behave like the master of the house. Moreover, he reserved the right to choose a new husband for his ex-wife. At best, this new husband would have attended French schools and universities; at worst, he would be nothing more than an old house servant, a Senegalese Tirailleur, or a frustrated military man, but who got along well with the rooster, to whom he vowed to keep careful watch over his former home.

With time, the new husband would become temperamental, would build castles for himself, proclaim himself "General in his Labyrinth," president for life—or even in death—with a cane and traditional uniform. And we are the children of this divorce who must be understood.

You would have spoken today in particular to the former colonies of black, French-speaking Africa, Jimmy. These are undoubtedly the only ones since the "The Suns of Independence," since the refrain from Grand Kallé's song, "Indépendence Cha Cha," who remain on the platforms, deceived, and cheated, watching the phantom trains passing, bemoaning the cursed Ham. How will they not yield to the lure of the "competition for victimhood?"

I am sure that it would be to them that you would address your words, though not to scold them, but to look them in the eyes.

You would tell them that the attitude of the eternal victim could not for much longer absolve them of their inaction, their equivocation.

You would tell them that their current condition stems, directly or indirectly, from their own illusions, confusion, and their one-sided reading of history.

There is nothing worse than the person who plays the role he is expected to play, aiding even the most mediocre of directors to exploit his own despair. The world is now full of this type of artist short on ideas, and it has been a long while since the plight of the Negro inspired anyone's altruism. His salvation is to be found neither in commiseration nor in aid. If that were all that was required, the wretched of the earth would have changed the course of history.

For me to say "Negro" is no longer enough to evoke in the mind of the other the memory of centuries-long humiliation endured by my people.

It is no longer enough, Jimmy, for me to say I am from the South to get assistance from the North in their third-world effort, because I know that aid is nothing more than a veiled prolonging of enslavement, and to be black no longer means anything, starting with people of color themselves. Moreover, Frantz Fanon finishes *Black Skin, White Masks* in terms that should inspire us in our understanding of our own condition: "I do not want to fall victim to the black world's ruse. My life does not have to be a summary of negro values. [. . .] I am not a prisoner of history. I do not have search through it to give meaning to my destiny . . . In the world into which I direct my own step, I create myself endlessly."[136]

Instead of seeking out the definition of one's status, one is better served by interpreting and untangling the meaning of words, what they convey, what they imply, for the destiny of the person of color. In the end, definitions imprison us, take away from us the ability to create ourselves endlessly, to imagine a different world. As long as these definitions appear absolute, the question of the other remains acute. It is in this vein that I understand your warning: "And, in fact, the truth about the black man, as a historical entity and as a human being, *has* been hidden from him, deliberately and cruelly; the power of the white world is threatened whenever a black man refuses to accept the white world's definitions."[137]

* * *

In 2004 Albert Memmi published *Portrait du décolonisé arabo-musulman et de quelques autres*, in which he tasked himself with assessing the condition of the formerly colonized, a half century after the "Suns of Independence." This work shows us to what extent the offspring of immigrants, having lost their cultural bearings, invent themselves by espousing other forms of culture that are now the subject of many studies. The children of immigrants live in a sort of social exclusion that ultimately drives them to delinquency, as Memmi highlights. Disoriented, they turn to the culture of your native country—I should say: to black American culture—that some consider to be a subculture, with all the negative associations that come along with that: "Having refused to identify with his parents, believing himself to be rejected by the majority, nothing remains for the son of the immigrant but to exist on his own. He must therefore seek a model to emulate outside of mainstream society, and outside of its borders [. . .] Naturally he will not look to foreign conservatives, with whom he would experience the same type of rejection. Rather, he gravitates toward the opposition and the marginalized, to what one refers to as the 'subculture,' preferably American, and principally black culture."[138]

The son of the immigrant who "borrows" from black American subculture creates a status for himself not unlike the one you experienced as a black American in Europe: you came from somewhere, yet Europe was not interested in your roots. Except here we have the son of the immigrant who does not see that the black subculture he chooses has for a long while been an expression of the need to return to the mythic land in the eyes of the black American: Africa.

The immigrant's son, Memmi continues, "still doesn't know, believing he is borrowing from the blacks, that the blacks sought their inspiration in Africa, not only because of their common skin color, but because, judging themselves to still be under the yoke of whites, after having been their slaves, they believe they have in this way found their pre-oppression origins."[139]

In this way subculture is a reflex, a refuge, for an entire group that considers itself to be the victim of marginalization. They participate in a mob mentality and a collective desire to reject the mainstream vision of the world. Anyone who rises against the west is a hero for these minorities. We saw this, Jimmy, in the wake of events that changed the face of the world on September 11, 2001.

Finally, through the invention of their own language and style of dressing derived from African-Americans, the young immigrants wear these differences as badges of their revolt. They defy law enforcement who, in their minds, look at them as lifelong "Natives of the Republic". . .

afterword

dialogue with Ralph,
the invisible man

Yesterday I walked the length of Santa Monica Beach in hopes of crossing the vagabond to whom I dedicated this Letter to Jimmy. I hadn't seen him in some time, and I began to worry.

I asked the ice-cream vendor if he had seen this character, easily recognizable by the bundle of clothes on his back. But the vendor had not seen him in some while, either.

So I walked back up toward Ocean Boulevard and sat down at a table on the terrace of Ma'kai, my manuscript in hand. I intended to read over the first few pages of the text since, in several days, I would have to send it off to the editor in France. But I could not do it without finding the wanderer.

* * *

I was immersed in my reading when the sound of a horn startled me.

Lifting my head, I nearly jumped for joy: *my* wanderer was crossing the street, the "don't walk" sign still flashing red. He approached Ma'Kai.

I stood up and waved to him. He looked away, hastening his step toward Santa Monica Boulevard. I quickly paid my bill and tried to follow him. Near a big hotel, I saw him sit down on a bench and open his bundle of clothing. From the disorder of his belongings, he pulled out a book: *Invisible Man*, by Ralph Ellison . . .

I took out a five dollar bill and handed it to him, as a pretext for striking up a conversation.

"You take me for a beggar, too? I see, I see," he said.

"Actually, I . . ."

"Don't apologize. Please. —Sit down."

"You like Ralph Ellison," I asked, to change the subject.

"I read him every day. If I had a bed, I'd say that it was my 'bedside reading.' Let's say that it's my beach reading, or, better yet, my sand reading. On top of it, my name is Ralph, too, so it's almost like I wrote the book."

"I haven't seen you again at Santa Monica Beach, Ralph."

"But I see *you* every day."

"Oh really?"

"I even know where you live."

"How's that? You're joking, Ralph!"

"It's a long story."

"Can't we talk about it now?"

"No, I don't feel like it . . . Just know that you live in my old apartment."

I remained speechless, simultaneously skeptical and gripped by a sudden distress.

"You think I'm crazy, is that it?" he asked.

"You have to admit that . . ."

"Ask around and come back to see me."

"I haven't seen you in quite awhile!"

"Oh, sometimes I change locations. Last month I dreamed that people were attacking me here. So I went out around Venice Beach to get some rest. It's nice there, but there are too many people. People also trample my sandcastles and I can't read my Ralph Ellison in peace."

"But sometimes you destroy your sandcastles yourself."

"So? I'm the one who built them! I have the right to do what I want with my castles. I just can't tolerate people coming to destroy them. They don't realize how much time it takes me to build them."

"I'd like to talk to you about someone—an author. This year is the twentieth anniversary of his death . . ."

"James Baldwin?"

"How do you know that?"

"It's written right there, on the paper you're holding. And I see his picture there, too."

"Oh, right . . . Actually I've just dedicated my *Letter to Jimmy* to you, the text that I'll publish in France in honor of the author who lived there."

"No kidding! But why would you dedicate it to me? I've never read Baldwin."

"I'll give you one of his books tomorrow."

"Don't bother, I only read Ralph Ellison. The others aren't my thing."

"But why Ralph Ellison?"

"Because I'm an invisible man, too. I'm white, but I'm really black . . . And since I'm a white man, people don't see me; they don't see my misery because I'm part of the majority. So for a long time I've lived this way, hoping that God would give me my true skin color one day."

"I don't understand . . ."

"You can't understand. Come see me tomorrow."

"Where?"

"At one of my castles, I will tell you about the place you live. You will know the whole story, and I'll show you things."

"What time?"

"Four o'clock. By the way, don't forget to bring me one of James Baldwin's books."

postscript

James Baldwin
the brother, the father

The paths that lead us to a writer are as mysterious as the ways of the Lord. Several years ago, I was far from imagining that I would one day "talk" with the American author James Baldwin, who died in the south of France in 1987, in Saint-Paul-de-Vence. I was not drawn to him because we had the same color skin. I was born in Africa, the land of his ancestors. I had lived in France, his land of refuge. And now I live in his homeland: America. Was this reason enough to devote my admiration to him, even though most of the writers I admire often have nothing to do with Africa, France or America? Was I simply in awe before a writer whose uncommon path and chaotic life could not help but move me? More than this, the life of every author is often its own novel, sometimes even a tragic one. This is perhaps why the genre of biography exists . . .

And so, in 2007, on the twentieth anniversary of Baldwin's passing, I devoted a book to him—*Letter to Jimmy*. As I wrote this "love letter," I had the feeling that Baldwin was reading the manuscript over my shoulder, without really interfering in the process. At most, he may have been smiling when I lost myself in my theories, or when I surrendered to the notions I had formed while reading his work. His writing encompasses most literary genres with a dazzling skill that made Jimmy one of the most important figures in American literature. This diverse body of work quickly projected the author of *Go Tell It on the Mountain* to the intellectual forefront of his country's civil rights movement, with an intensity and a sense of commitment that can be summed up in this phrase from his essay "The Fire Next Time:" "To act is to be committed, and to be committed is to be in danger." At the same time, the themes Baldwin explored in his various novels go beyond the limits of race, such as in *Giovanni's Room* where one notices the absence of the "Negro question," where taboos are shattered by evoking homosexuality, where there are only white characters, and in a plot that unfolds in Europe—France in particular—not in America as in the novels of his colleagues of that period (Richard Wright, Chester Himes . . .). This type of approach was risky at a time when, in Africa as well as in black America, an author of color was expected to champion the black cause and the idea of "negritude," in vogue in Paris, too, the gathering place for most American intellectuals threatened by racial segregation. Baldwin retaliated against this type of socially mandated literature, and in this way his stance enticed me.

If I imagined Baldwin coughing slightly from time to time when I was writing *Letter to Jimmy*, or imagined his footsteps near my library, I would lift my eyes and see before me the photo taped to the wall, in front of my desk. This photo is essentially the source of our encounter. I had bought it in the late 80s from a *bouquinistes*, a used bookseller's kiosk, along the Seine. Baldwin had looked at me then as if he were begging me to save him from his public display. The bookseller shared with me the information that he had known the author, whom he had seen walking around "over there"—he pointed to the Place Saint-Michel. Should I have believed him? I bought the photo and walked down into a Metro station . . .

Sitting in the Metro, I studied Baldwin's features closely. I was half dozing. My own life appeared to me now in black and white, like the image. I had the feeling that I had known this man, that I had met him in the old quarters of Pointe-Noire, in Congo. He had the face of the brother I would have liked to have had, and of the biological father I had never known—Baldwin had not known his father either, a fact that played an undeniably major role in his work. In essence I was asking Baldwin to adopt me, to take my hand, to lead me to "another country" where "no one knows my name." And so I invented for myself a brother in his image, and a father in his image. Alas, I would discover that he would make David, his main character in *Giovanni's Room*, say: "People can't, unhappily, invent their mooring posts, their lovers and their friends, anymore than they can invent their parents. Life gives these and also takes them away and the great difficulty is to say Yes to life." These words echo through my thoughts still today. The destruction they inflicted on my imaginary world was similar to that endured by a kid to whom it has been suddenly revealed that Santa Claus does not exist. To console myself at the time, I tucked Baldwin's image between the pages of books I was reading, whether they were written by him or by others. In this way we were reading the same books and we were traveling together. Much later—I had already moved to the United States—I came upon the same image in a bookstore in a new edition of one of Baldwin's novels. I no longer felt the same as I once had in France, since my image of him now hid a story behind it, a chance encounter that could not be reproduced . . .

Every time I look again at "my" photo, my eyes linger on the wrinkles of Baldwin's face. They are furrows, footpaths I have to follow in order to make my way to the clearing where I might hear his voice, where he might share with me at last the secrets he did not reveal during his lifetime. His smile is faint, and changes as often as I try to describe it. But his eyes, most of all! "Those big eyes—prominent on your face, that once mocked your father, unaware that they would later peer into souls, or that they would pierce through the darkest part of humanity, before closing forever—still hold their power to search deeply, even from the next life," I would write, at the beginning of my *Letter to Jimmy* . . .

I situate Baldwin's novel *Giovanni's Room* at the peak of his creative production, and *The Fire Next Time* at the height of his thought as a champion of civil rights. With it, Baldwin changed my previous understanding of the world. After reading *The Fire Next Time*, you can no longer look at society in the same way. What, after all, does Baldwin teach us if not that desperation, internal agony and "the unbearable lightness of being" haunt all races? From there, the writer must invent—or even reinvent—a universe in which neighborly love is our only salvation, since none of us can hide from the inevitable truth: "Life is tragic simply because the earth turns and the sun inexorably rises and sets, and one day, for each of us, the sun will go down for the last, last time." Baldwin based his dream on the redemption of human nature, on reclaiming what we lost a long time ago: the beauty of life. When all is said and done, what can inspire us more than these words? "Perhaps the whole root of our trouble, the human trouble, is that we will sacrifice all the beauty of our lives, will imprison ourselves in totems, taboos, crosses, blood sacrifices, steeples, mosques, races, armies, flags, nations, in order to deny the fact of death, the only fact we have."

Alain Mabanckou

endnotes

1. James Baldwin, "The Fire Next Time" in *Collected Essays of James Baldwin*, ed. Toni Morrison (New York: Library of America, 1998), 334-5.
2. Ibid., 334-5.
3. Ibid., 334-5.
4. James Baldwin, "Notes of a Native Son" in *Collected Essays of James Baldwin*, ed. Toni Morrison (New York: Library of America, 1998), 42.
5. Ibid., 42.
6. James Baldwin, *Conversations with James Baldwin*, eds. Fred Standley and Louis H. Pratt (Jackson: University Press of Mississippi, 1989), 77-78.
7. Ibid., 199.
8. David Leeming, *James Baldwin: A Biography* (New York: Knopf, Distributed by Random House, 1994), 3.
9. Benoît Depardieu, *James Baldwin* (Paris: Belin, 2004), 20-21.
10. "Notes of a Native Son," op. cit., 13.
11. Ibid., p. 68.
12. Leeming, op. cit, 6.
13. Standley and Pratt, op. cit, 78.
14. Ibid., 161.
15. James Campbell, *Talking at the Gates: A Life of James Baldwin* (New York: Penguin Books, 1991), 10.
16. Ibid., p. 40.
17. Ibid., p. 37.

18. Ibid., p. 38.
19. "Notes of a Native Son," op. cit., 9.
20. "The Fire Next Time," op. cit., 307.
21. Ibid., 309.
22. Ibid., 307.
23. "Notes of a Native Son," op. cit., 75.
24. Ibid, 64.
25. "The Fire Next Time," op. cit., 291.
26. "Notes of a Native Son," op. cit., 66.
27. Depardieu, op. cit., p. 17.
28. Leeming, op. cit., 17.
29. "The Fire Next Time," op. cit., 327.
30. Ibid., p. 14.
31. "Notes of a Native Son," op. cit., 6.
32. Michel Fabre, *La Rive noire: les écrivains noirs américains à Paris, 1830-1995* (Marseille: André Dimanche, 1999), 71.
33. "Notes of a Native Son," op. cit., 9.
34. Robert Coles, "James Baldwin Back Home," *New York Times*, July 31, 1977.
35. Ibid.
36. James Campbell, *Exiled in Paris: Richard Wright, James Baldwin, Samuel Beckett and Others on the Left Bank* (Berkeley: University of California Press, 2003), 24.
37. Hazel Rowley, *Richard Wright: The Life and Times* (New York: Henry Holt, 2003).
38. James Baldwin, "Nobody Knows My Name" in *Collected Essays of James Baldwin*, ed. Toni Morrison (New York: Library of America, 1998), 259.
39. Leeming, op. cit., 49.
40. "Notes of a Native Son," op. cit., 5.
41. Leeming, op. cit., 52-53.
42. Campbell, *Exiled in Paris*, op. cit., 24.
43. Benoît Depardieu, op. cit., 28–29 (quotation drawn from "Nobody Knows My Name" and translated into French by Benoît Depardieu in his book. The exact source of Depardieu's original English citation of Baldwin's work is unclear).
44. "Notes of a Native Son," op. cit., 11-18.
45. Ibid., p. 20.

46. Amanda Claybaugh, Introduction and Notes to *Uncle Tom's Cabin,* by Harriet Beecher Stowe (New York: Barnes & Noble Classics, 2003), xxxvi.

47. *Notes of a Native Son,* op. cit., 12.

48. Depardieu, op. cit., 80.

49. Claybaugh, op. cit., xiv–xv.

50. Ibid., xviii.

51. *Notes of a Native Son,* op. cit., 16.

52. Ibid., p. 23-24.

53. Claybaugh, op. cit., xxxii.

54. "Notes of a Native Son," op. cit., 19-35.

55. Ibid., 30.

56. Ibid., 27.

57. Ibid., 27.

58. Campbell, *Exiled in Paris,* op. cit., 31.

59. *Collected Essays,* op. cit., p. 258.

60. Ibid., p. 260.

61. Langston Hughes, review of *Notes of a Native Son,* by James Baldwin, *New York Times,* February 26, 1958.

62. Campbell, *Exiled in Paris,* op. cit., 29.

63. Camara Laye, *L'Enfant noir* (Paris: Plon, 1954). New Plon 2006 edition with preface by the author, Alain Mabanckou.

64. Eza Boto, *Ville cruelle* (Paris: Présence africaine, 1954); *Le Pauvre Christ de Bomba* (Paris: Présence africaine, 1956).

65. Aimé Césaire, *Cahier d'un retour au pays natal* (Paris: Présence africaine, 1983).

66. Mongo Beti, "Enfant noir," *Présence Africaine,* 1954.

67. Lilyan Kesteloot, *Anthologie négro-africaine : panorama critique des prosateurs, poètes et dramaturges noirs du XXe siècle* (Vanves: Edicef, 1987).

68. Simon Njami, *James Baldwin, ou, Le devoir de violence* (Paris: Seghers, 1991).

69. Campbell, *Talking at the Gates,* op. cit., 71.

70. Dwight A. McBride, "The Parvenu Baldwin and the Other Side of Redemption," in *James Baldwin Now* (New York: New York University Press, 1999), 234.

71. *Collected Essays,* op. cit., p. 594-600.

72. Ibid., p. 597.

73. Ibid., p. 597.
74. James Baldwin, "Freaks and the American Ideal of Manhood," *Playboy*, January 1985, reproduced in *Collected Essays*, op. cit., 814-829.
75. *Collected Essays*, op. cit., p. 814.
76. Ibid., p. 815.
77. Faggot, a derogatory term for a homosexual man used at the time, which Wright himself would use against Baldwin.
78. *Collected Essays*, op. cit., p. 821.
79. Ibid., p. 820.
80. Campbell, *Exiled in Paris*, op. cit., 33.
81. Eldridge Cleaver, *Soul on Ice* (New York: Delta, 1999), 124. First edition published in 1967 by McGraw Hill, New York.
82. Paul Goodman, "Not Enough of a World to Grow in," *New York Times*, June 24, 1962.
83. Depardieu, op. cit., 80.
84. James Baldwin, *Another Country* (New York: Random House, 2013), p. 22.
85. Ibid., p. 27.
86. Leeming, op. cit., 56.
87. "Notes of a Native Son," op. cit., 42.
88. Ibid., 86.
89. Dominic Thomas, *Black France: colonialism, immigration, and transnationalism* (Bloomington: Indiana University Press, 2007), 10.
90. Ibid., p. 88.
91. "Notes of a Native Son," op. cit., 88.
92. Ibid., p. 150.
93. Frantz Fanon, *Peau noire, masques blancs* (Paris: Seuil, 1952), 179.
94. "The Fire Next Time," op. cit., 342.
95. Leeming, op. cit., 121-122.
96. Campbell, *Talking at the Gates*, op. cit., 109.
97. Césaire, op. cit., 22-23.
98. Sheldon Binn, review of *The Fire Next Time*, by James Baldwin, *New York Times*, January 31, 1963.
99. "The Fire Next Time," op. cit., 340.
100. Ibid., p. 134-135.

101. Frantz Fanon, *Les Damnés de la terre* (Paris: Gallimard, "Folio," 1991), 43.
102. "The Fire Next Time," op. cit., 346.
103. Ibid., p. 135.
104. Alan Stoskopf, "The Murder of Emmett Till: A Series of Four Lessons," *https://www.facinghistory.org/for-educators/educator-resources/lessons-and-units/emmett-till-series-four-lessons*
105. Walter Meserve in *The Black American Writer: Vol.II Poetry and Drama,* ed. C.W.E. Bigsby (Baltimore: Penguin Books, 1969), as reproduced by Chip Lockwood in "Baldwin's 'Blues' remain powerful, 37 years later," *Yale Herald Online,* 2001. http://www.yaleherald.com/archive/xxxi/2001.03.30/ae/p21baldwin.html
106. "Notes of a Native Son," op. cit., 49.
107. Ibid., 49.
108. James Baldwin, "Negroes Are Anti-Semitic Because They're Anti-White," *New York Times*, April 9, 1967.
109. Ibid.
110. Ibid.
111. Ibid.
112. "Notes of a Native Son," op. cit., 50.
113. Ibid., 50.
114. Budd Schulberg, *La Forêt interdite*: suivi de *L'Atelier d'écriture de Watts* et de *Dialogue en noir et blanc*, (Paris: Rivages Poche, 2004), 280-282. Original American title: *Wind Across the Everglades*.
115. Ibid., p. 281.
116. Ibid., p. 283.
117. Baldwin, "Negroes Are Anti-Semitic Because They're Anti-White," op. cit.
118. Ibid.
119. Émile Frèche, *La Mort d'un pote* (Paris: Éditions Panama, 2006).
120. *Le Nouvel Observateur*, March 25, 2006.
121. Ibid.
122. Dominic Thomas, *Black France*, op. cit., 10.
123. Frantz Fanon, *Peau noire, masques blancs*, op. cit., 185-186.
124. Leeming op. cit., 77.

125. Campbell, *Talking at the Gates*, op. cit., 239.

126. Ibid., p. 240.

127. Ibid., p. 282.

128. Ibid., p. 281.

129. Quincy Troupe, *James Baldwin: The Legacy* (New York: Simon and Schuster, 1989).

130. Campbell, *Talking at the Gates*, op. cit., 281.

131. Pascal Bruckner, *Le Sanglot de l'homme blanc. Tiers-monde, culpabilité, haine de soi* (Paris: Seuil, 1983), and, more recently, *La Tyrannie de la pénitence : essai sur le masochisme occidental* (Paris: Grasset, 2006).

132. Bruckner, preface to his own book, *Sanglot de l'homme blanc* (Paris: Seuil, "Points," 2002), iv.

133. Jean-Paul Sartre, preface to *Damnés de la terre,* by Frantz Fanon (Paris: Gallimard "Folio," 1991), 42.

134. Ibid., p. 41.

135. Achille Mbembe, in an article entitled "Francophonie et politique du monde," that appeared on the author's website (www.alainmabanckou.net), March 24, 2007.

136. Frantz Fanon, *Peau noire, masques blancs*, op.cit., 186.

137. "The Fire Next Time," op. cit., 326.

138. Albert Memmi, *Portrait du décolonisé arabo-musulman et de quelques autres* (Paris: Gallimard, 2004), 141-142.

139. Ibid., p. 142.